⇥ ESSENTIAL ⇤
WRITING SKILLS
FOR COLLEGE
& BEYOND

C.M. GILL

WD
WRITER'S DIGEST
BOOKS

WRITER'S DIGEST
BOOKS

An imprint of Penguin Random House LLC
penguinrandomhouse.com

ISBN 9781599637594
eBook ISBN 9781599637655

Printed in the United States of America

Cover design by Bethany Rainbolt
Interior design by Rob Warnick

⤏ Acknowledgments ⤎

I would like to express my gratitude to those who helped bring this project to fruition, especially my students for inspiring me with the idea of this book: Thank you for your dedication to writing and learning, and for making my work feel not at all like work.

To the many teachers who taught me to write, to think, and to learn, without whom this book would not exist: Thank you Ms. Urias, Mrs. Hall, Mrs. Watson, Mrs. Grigsby, Mr. Quisenberry, Mr. Proctor, Dr. Cohen, Professor Rosenberg, Professor Beebe, and Professor Wilson. Special thanks to Professor Robin Gallaher Branch.

To my colleagues and friends for supporting and encouraging me to persevere: Thank you David Borden, Katherine Dowdy, Patricia Hernandez, Dolores Collins, Nadine Cooper-Kohn, Mary Helen Martinez, Jason Katz, Tonya Lyles, Ted Rachofsky, Jason Brown, David Zuniga, Dr. Dorado Kinney, Sunita Misra, and Lisa Carlo.

Thank you to Austin Community College, EBSCO, and Innovative Interfaces for the use of their screenshots. Thank you to The Center for Enhanced Teaching and Learning at The University of New Brunswick for the use of their sample grading rubric.

Thank you to my editors and the team at Writer's Digest and Penguin Random House: Rachel Randall, Stephen Ryan, and Joanna Ng. Without your help and insight, this book might still be lying dormant in a drawer.

To my family who supported me during this and all other endeavors always and without question: To my friend and sister, Kim; my father and teacher, Charles; my uncle, Larry; and my wonderfully stellar but growing-up-much-too-quickly nephews, Tyler, Alex, Dylan, and Silas.

Thank you to my mother, Robin, who is always my first, loudest, and greatest supporter; I couldn't have written any of this without you. Thank you for always being there and never giving up on me.

And thank you to Thomas, who listened to me blather on about this book and many others: Thank you for your sympathetic ear, your patience, your belief in me, and your unyielding support and encouragement.

➤ About the Author ◄

C. M. Gill has taught academic writing courses for almost twenty years, in both university and community college environments. She has published, presented, and won awards for her own academic work at national and international conferences. She is the author of the bestselling *College Success for Adults: Insider Tips for Effective Learning* and currently serves on the faculty at Austin Community College in Austin, Texas.

Contents

Foreword

This book began in my university writing classes. My students complained about their enormous, all-inclusive writing manual. They felt intimidated and overwhelmed by it, and they asked instead for a concise, easy-to-understand guide to the college writing process. This book *is* that guide. The organization will take you through the writing process—from generating ideas to polishing the final product.

The value of mastering this process simply cannot be overestimated. In college, almost all assessment is *written*. Professors in every discipline test students' ability not only to learn the material but also to demonstrate this knowledge in writing. Aside from the major papers assigned, college professors also require in-class essays, book reviews, and chapter summaries, and even multiple-choice exams include short-answer and essay questions designed to test writing skills. In fact, as a college student, you can expect to write thousands, if not millions, of words in your undergraduate career. Strong writing skills are also crucial in the professional world. Businesses, governments, and organizations of all kinds highly value those rare people who possess the skills and knowledge to communicate effectively in writing. Clearly, investing in improving your writing skills is not only a good idea; it's crucial.

This book will empower you with a strong knowledge of the college writing process and fill any gaps within your knowledge of spelling, grammar, or punctuation. Feel free to use the book as you see fit; skip ahead to access the material you feel you most need, or read the book cover to cover. As with anything else, practice will improve your abilities, so write as much and as often as you can. If you would like more practice than is offered within the pages of this book, you can access additional practice quizzes and student examples for free online at www .writersdigest.com/essential-college-writing.

Best of luck to you, and happy writing!

ⵢⵞ Introduction ⵞⵢ

UNDERSTANDING ACADEMIA

You've probably heard people refer to the college campus as "The Ivory Tower." This is, in some ways, an accurate description of the world and people you will encounter in college. The atmosphere is one of idealism, of the pursuit of knowledge, and of the quest for higher ideals. Mundane, practical matters hold significantly less importance here than in, say, the business world. In academia, the dollar is not paramount, nor is physical appearance, and markers of status, such as expensive clothing, accessories, and various other products, are not essential to success.

In academia, there is a purposeful disconnect from the so-called everyday world, especially in the departments of the humanities (psychology, English, philosophy, music, theater, and so on). In fact, the pursuit of higher knowledge requires this disconnect because it requires you to take on a different mindset than the one in the current mainstream or "everyday world."

It is important that you begin to cultivate and understand this mindset. Why? The people and texts you will encounter in your college career will probably be unlike any you have ever encountered, and it can be disorienting if you feel unsure about your role as a student and the purpose of your work. However, this world is not as difficult to navigate as you may think, for it has but one central principle at its core, and once you understand that principle, you can and will excel in academia.

What is this central principle? Consider for a moment why college professors *become* college professors (instead of, say, accountants or lawyers or dentists). All professors were once college students, and most remained in academia because they fell in love with the search for knowledge, the inquiry into what is known and true, and the desire to find definitive answers. They remain there because they want to continue this quest and meet and work with others who share that goal.

Keep this point in mind as you write your papers and attend your courses because it illustrates the central principle of academia and the base on which it is built: the quest for knowledge.

If you think this principle of "the quest for knowledge" sounds high-minded and philosophical, you're right; it is. However, it is also a fact—and if you remember and apply it, you will succeed in college. To be successful in college means to reflect in your work this desire *to know and to prove*.

Remember, academics value, above all, knowledge. Professors seek to examine, to learn, to explain, and to know. They have dedicated their lives not to the pursuit of money, fame, or prestige but rather to the pursuit of knowledge, and they expect their students to seek and present such knowledge as well.

The best way to impress an academic is to illustrate that you understand and respect this principle and that you, too, seek higher, deeper knowledge.

How do you go about doing that?

> *In your writing, do not merely rehash known information on the assigned topic, subject, or person. Instead, examine, question, and challenge information, theories, and interpretations. Do this, and you will excel in your college classes.*

If you're thinking this point is easier said than done, you are right. However, it's not as difficult as you think. It begins with taking your role as a student seriously, and clearly you already do or you wouldn't have taken the time to read this book.

While proofreading and editing your work is undoubtedly important, as you write, keep in mind this larger picture of the quest for knowledge and focus on *it*, rather than on tiny grammar or spelling errors. Ask yourself what you seek to discover on any assignment, and *truly try to find it. This desire to understand will be evident in your work, and it will not go unrewarded.* Any small errors in punctuation or grammar that you make will seem minor and will likely be forgiven if at the heart of your work stands a writer who obviously holds a deep respect for the quest for knowledge.

UNDERSTANDING THE ACADEMIC ESSAY

Many students have heard horror stories from friends or older siblings about college essays requiring "research" or "scholarly sources," and many students enter their classes with one fearful question: "Will we have to do research?" The answer is almost always yes— but don't let research scare you.

Professors do *not* expect you to know every text or idea within a certain topic—and certainly not within an entire field (such as biology, literature, or philosophy). Your instructors *will* expect you to show respect for the quest for knowledge by demonstrating within your work that you have read and understand other key scholars' ideas.

The essence of the college essay contains three major parts; be sure your essays contain all three:

- Your ideas
- Their (other scholars') ideas
- The connections between your ideas and their ideas

Or, if you think mathematically, imagine this as an equation:

Your Ideas + Their Ideas + Connections Between Your Ideas and Their Ideas = Successful College Essay

Tackle each of these parts one at a time. Most students find the entire writing process to be much easier when they move from one part to the next rather than trying to simultaneously complete all three parts. In fact, the organization of this book reflects and illustrates this principle.

You'll notice this book begins with helping you develop your own ideas first. However, this organization is not to suggest you *must* begin every essay with this step. Some students prefer to do research first and then develop their own ideas. Try both methods and see which works better for you.

ACING THE ACADEMIC ESSAY

Regardless of the type of writing your instructors assign, remember that a successful academic writer aims to achieve two goals: It should be both *credible* and *interesting*.

These two aims are indeed listed in order of importance; if you cannot write an engaging, interesting essay, then at least be sure to write a credible one.

To write a *credible* essay:

- **ADDRESS AND ANSWER THE PROMPT.** Ensure your essay remains focused and on topic through each paragraph.
- **CITE THE WORK OF KEY THINKERS IN THE FIELD.** Consult your professor, librarian, or teaching assistant to find out who these people are and how to correctly cite them.
- **GO ABOVE AND BEYOND THE CALL OF THE ASSIGNMENT.** If the instructor does not require outside sources but you include and properly cite them anyway, you and your work will stand out as superior.
- **PROOFREAD.** Do not have spelling, grammatical, typographical, or punctuation errors.
- **GO TO OFFICE HOURS.** Speak directly with your professor to show you take the class seriously.

To write an *interesting* essay:

- **BE CONTROVERSIAL.** Take a different stand than other writers (especially your classmates).
- **EXPERIMENT WITH YOUR WRITING STYLE.** Vary your sentence structure and word choice, and don't be afraid to experiment and take risks; often, innovation is well worth the risk.
- **CONSIDER—AND CHALLENGE—THE ASSUMPTIONS AND THEORIES OF OTHERS.** Successful academic writing requires engaging with the ideas of others, not just presenting your own. It is crucial that you learn how to consider and respond to others' work.

Granted, some of these strategies can be risky, and not all professors will admire your attempt to experiment with language or form, debunk their favorite scholar's theory, or write about a controversial topic. If you're planning on experimenting or being controversial, show your instructor your draft during office hours. You'll be able to tell immediately if they find it distasteful. If so, tuck it away and save it for another semester. If not, feel free to proceed.

HOW TO GET STARTED

THE STUDENT-FIRST VS. THE SCHOLARS-FIRST MODEL

Many students struggle with beginning the writing process. Essentially, two models exist that can help you begin: the student-first or the scholars-first models. Choose one or both of the following strategies to help develop your own ideas as well as find and incorporate the ideas of others into your essay.

THE STUDENT-FIRST MODEL

1. The student writes out and determines *their own* ideas on the topic first, without deeply considering the work of other scholars.
2. The student begins examining other scholars' ideas to compare and contrast those with their own. The student may or may not alter their original viewpoints, but they must include the work of others in their essay.

THE SCHOLARS-FIRST MODEL

1. The student examines *other scholars' ideas* before exploring their own to get a firm grasp on the major ideas or theories within the assigned topic or text.
2. The student focuses on developing their own opinions, beliefs, and evidence. The student may or may not agree with the scholars' ideas, but they must include them in their work.

WHICH MODEL IS BETTER?

The answer depends on the writer and perhaps on the topic. If you receive a topic you know absolutely nothing about, then you may want to try the second strategy. However, if you already have many ideas or opinions on the topic, then the first strategy may work better for you.

Most colleges and universities employ the "Scholars-First Model" in their classes. Instructors typically have students read the best and/or current research on a topic. Then, they require students to write a paper based on their understanding and/or opinion of that research and topic. Both models work, though, so try both and see which one works best for you.

TYPES OF ACADEMIC ESSAYS

In your high school classes, you may have written the following "types" of essays:

- Informative
- Persuasive
- How-to or instructional
- Personal or reflective
- Analytical
- Comparison/contrast

The good news is that the skills you gained in writing these essays won't go to waste; you'll absolutely use these abilities in your college writing classes. Keep in mind, however, that most of these essays do not exist singularly in the college environment as they did in the high school classroom. In other words, professors will *not* label the type of essay they assign; they will simply write an assignment, hand it out, and expect you to understand the assignment and complete it. The essays they assign probably won't focus on a single skill (such as comparison/contrast or persuasion).

> The typical college writing assignment requires all the skills employed in all the essay types learned in high school.

For example, a persuasive collegiate essay typically requires writers to inform, include, or build on personal anecdotes or experience, compare and contrast different scholars' opinions or theories, analyze research, *and* persuade.

Unless you attended a very progressive high school or GED program, this type of writing will probably be both new and challenging for you—

at first. Don't panic, though; writing is like most other tasks; with time and practice, it will get easier.

Also, remember that professors do *not* expect you to turn in an essay worthy of Shakespeare, Faulkner, or Plato, especially in a freshmen composition course. They *do* expect students to spend the necessary time ensuring their work meets the requirements of the assignment. If you feel uncertain about whether you have included all the necessary information, go to your professor's office hours and ask the instructor to look over your work. A simple office visit can mean the difference between an *A* or a *B* or even passing versus failing.

UNDERSTANDING THE PROMPT

The writing prompt is the set of instructions you receive from your instructor dictating the requirements of the assignment. The prompt tells you how to succeed on the assignment—and how to fail.

Most beginning students quickly read the prompt and then toss it aside in their fervor to get started on the essay. Don't commit this cardinal sin!

> *Don't just glance at the prompt, toss it aside, and never reread it again. Keep it with you as you write, and refer to it often.*

This advice is especially important because college writing prompts are sometimes complicated, long-winded, and downright persnickety. One quick read-through is probably not sufficient to fully and comprehensively understand the assignment.

Read the prompt carefully. Highlight or underline the key terms, and ask questions if necessary to make sure you fully understand the assignment before you actually start writing. Refer to the prompt as you write to ensure your work actually addresses the question(s) posed.

You might be surprised by how many students waste time writing a paper that does not meet the assignment. When these students receive their low—or even failing—score, they become frustrated not only with that particular assignment but with the class in general. Investing the time necessary to understand the assignment will actually save you time, not to mention frustration.

Specifically, make sure you understand (at minimum) the following:

- What type of writing is required? (Persuasive? Informative? Both?)
- What is the central question, issue, or problem you need to address?
- Do you need to include outside sources? What kind? (Books? Articles? Both?)
- What type of documentation style do you need to use? MLA (Modern Language Association)? APA (American Psychological Association)?
- How many quotes should you include from in-class readings?
- Do you turn in a physical copy or an electronic copy? Both?

In the following sample college-level writing assignment, notice that the instructor provides students with clear indicators (bold and underlined) of the most important elements of the prompt. Not all professors will take the time to make their assignments this clear. Many do, though, so pay particular attention to items bolded, underlined, or otherwise emphasized in a writing assignment.

PAPER 3

Topic #1: Depictions of Family in Contemporary American Media

Compare and contrast two characters from different texts playing similar familial roles (such as husband/father or wife/mother). <u>How does each text define the role through each character?</u> <u>**Why?**</u> Assume your reader is moderately familiar with the texts you examine; do not waste space in your essay explaining the concept or plot of the film or television show.

Include in your essay the following:

- **The specific texts and characters you will examine**
- **Relevant supporting evidence from the television program or film—<u>NO plot summaries</u>**
- **Discussion of how this particular depiction of mother, father, daughter, or son, etc. is significant**

The professor underlines and bolds the assignment's central question.

Note the small but bolded and thus important follow-up question: "Why?" Students must ensure their work addresses this question as well.

Pay particular attention to the special instructions listed near the end of the prompt; the professor has provided students with a checklist of specific items to include in the assignment. Use this checklist throughout the writing process, especially before turning it in, to make sure the paper does indeed meet the requirements. If your instructor does not provide such a list, ask politely if she would consider providing one.

→ PART I →
IDEA-GENERATION

CHAPTER 1

Getting Started and Developing Your Ideas

"Where do I start?"

Students ask this question more than any other, and it's definitely an understandable one. Indeed, for many writers, one of the hardest parts of writing is getting started.

Facing the blank page can be intimidating, especially when you know someone will grade your ability to write well. Yet, you have to start at some point, so I will pass on to you one of the most helpful pieces of advice I have received on writing: Begin by beginning.

If you think that sounds simple, you're right—and you're wrong. Beginning can be easy, but it can also be quite difficult. All writers, whether they are beginners or experts, experience blocks, so don't panic if you can't immediately think of a dozen ideas for your paper.

> *There are many ways to start writing a paper, but there is not one right way.*

You will find in this chapter several strategies that writers (from beginners to professionals) use to help them get started in the writing process. Use some or all of these strategies; one may work well for you on one assignment but not another. Use the ones that work best for you.

As you write, keep in mind that *the ultimate goal of any paper is to explain the topic to yourself.* Yes, professors assign papers because they must, but the goal of any assignment is to elicit student thought on a particular topic, text, or theory. Remember the base of academia: the quest for knowledge. When you can explain your theory to yourself so well that *you* fully understand it and could teach it to others, then you probably have composed an excellent essay.

How do you achieve this feat?

Remember, begin by beginning. Don't worry about whether what you have written is "good" or not; just write. You can edit and polish later. The important thing is to get started.

THE CRITIC

The Critic is one of the first barriers writers must face. It's that internal voice that tells us our writing is useless, embarrassingly bad drivel that does not deserve to see the light of day, let alone earn credit.

The Critic may manifest itself in the likeness of a former English teacher, a hard-to-please parent, or even yourself. The bad news is that The Critic's voice will not likely disappear, no matter how much or how long you write. The good news is that when used wisely, the voice of The Critic can actually help you become a better writer.

Jack Heffron, author of *The Writer's Idea Book*, suggests listening to the voice of The Critic, but only *after* the first draft is composed.

> When The Critic appears, ready to rip your work to shreds, assure him that he will have his say, **but not yet**. After the draft is completed, The Critic can offer feedback, but not before.

When you learn to control when and how The Critic addresses your work, he will become your friend rather than your enemy. As Heffron points out, The Critic is a necessary voice at times because he can push you to improve your work and increase your ability to recognize strong, powerful writing.

> When you hear the voice of The Critic telling you your idea is stupid, your writing dull and pedestrian, tell the voice to wait. He may indeed be right. And he will have his turn, you promise, but it's not his turn now. The early draft is no place for The Critic. If he insists on interfering, try not to fight him directly. Instead, observe the voice, name it "The Critic," and let it go. .... Send him to a movie or on a nature hike or into the other room. He'll probably

> pop his head in from time to time, asking, 'Ready for me yet?' In as
> kind a voice as you can muster, simply say, "Not yet." (Heffron 19)

So, give The Critic his say, but only when you are ready to edit and revise—not when you are just beginning. His help is only required *after* you've composed.

Consider, for example, the case of Stephen King and his now-famous novel *Carrie*. This world-famous, award-winning writer of fiction and nonfiction books, as well as several short-story collections, apparently had a rough case of The Critic, too. Before he was famous, before he won any awards, he doubted his abilities just like the rest of us. In fact, his inner critic assessed *Carrie* and determined it so entirely useless that King finally just tossed it into the garbage.

Luckily, King's wife fished it out and encouraged him to keep working on it. This decision garnered him his first publication, which led to another and another, and eventually to fame, wealth, and a decades-long writing career—and all from a story his inner critic told him to scrap. This trashed story, in fact, has since been adapted into feature films, a television film, and even a musical. Not bad for "garbage."

If King had listened to The Critic's harsh judgments, he would probably not be the rich, successful, famous writer he is today. Instead, he temporarily silenced this voice and later used it to his advantage to improve the work. You can, too, if you learn to control your Critic.

> *Never let The Critic talk you out of writing. Only let him help you improve what you have already written.*

Great and successful writing begins with getting ideas onto the page or screen. You can go back and polish, delete, tinker, and improve later.

Remember, allow The Critic to have his say only when you are ready to edit and revise. (For more on controlling The Critic, see chapter 8.)

On the next few pages, you'll find several brainstorming and freewriting ideas that will help you to do just that—get started and generate ideas that will lead to full-length essays. Don't worry about the strength or brilliance of your ideas at this point. Simply write. Generate the ideas first. Revise and edit later.

FREEWRITING

You've probably practiced freewriting before, either in your personal writing, in high school, or in college classes. Freewriting is exactly what it sounds like: writing freely. Write whatever comes to mind, in whatever order it comes. Don't censor. Just write.

Some writers believe speed is the key to this technique. They believe writing as quickly as possible works best. If writing quickly works for you, then by all means do it. If you prefer to write at your regular pace, then try that as well.

> *The key to freewriting is to write without stopping and without censorship. This means you simply write without worrying about grammar, spelling, punctuation, logic, organization, and so on. All that matters is that you allow the ideas to flow. Absolutely no censorship. Editing comes later.*

If you think the idea is stupid, write it anyway. If the idea seems off-topic, write it anyway. If you get stuck, keep writing anyway; even if you write, "This is stupid; this isn't working. I can't think of anything to say," eventually ideas will begin to flow as your mind realizes it has free creative rein.

Try this strategy both with pen and paper *and* on the computer to see which method works best for you.

Remember, the aim of freewriting is to get your ideas onto the paper or screen. You can't do that if you're thinking about the quality or scope of the ideas, so try not to judge or evaluate as you write. Let your ideas flow onto the page or screen. You'll have plenty of time to delete, edit, or revise later.

If you tend to be a highly critical or perfectionist writer, this task may be difficult. But keep in mind that you will not be turning in this portion of the paper, and there is always time for refining and buffing later.

FREEWRITING STRATEGIES

FOCUSED FREEWRITING: Sit down with a blank page or screen. Focus your attention on your assignment, topic, or prompt. Write nonstop for at least five minutes (ten to fifteen minutes seems to work well for most people) without censoring or judging your ideas except to remain focused on your topic. As long as the idea relates to your topic, write it down— even if it doesn't seem very worthwhile initially. Stop when you run out of language, your hand cramps, or you run out of ink. Repeat as desired.

FREE FREEWRITING: Sit down with a blank page or screen in front of you and start writing. Write whatever comes to mind, whether it pertains to your topic or not. Just write. The ideas or worries swimming around in your mind will be released onto the page, and once this release occurs, your mind is free to unleash the depths of its abilities. Stop when you cannot write another word, the keys on your computer are stuck due to overuse, or your brain has decided to shut down. Repeat as desired.

TIMED FREEWRITING: Sit down with a blank page or screen. Set your phone, kitchen timer, or watch for a specific time. Some writers prefer five-minute increments, others twenty or more minutes, but try to work for at least five minutes. You can increase the time as you get better with this technique. Write freely or focus your writing on a specific topic; just write nonstop without censoring or judging your ideas until your timer releases you. Repeat as desired.

Note the difference between "focused" and "timed" freewriting: When you complete the former, you must remain focused on your topic; when you try the latter, you simply write and allow *any* ideas that occur to you to have free expression—even if these ideas initially seem off-topic. They may be, or they may not. Just write, and see what happens.

If you are writing about two time periods, theories, books, or paintings in a single paper, it can help to do a timed freewriting session for each. For example, if you have to analyze two characters, choose one to focus on first and write or type the character's name at the top of the page. Then while timing yourself, write everything you can think of about your subject. Once your time expires for that character or theme, repeat the process for the other one(s). This process works with multiple ideas, theories, paintings, historical figures, and the like.

WORD-ASSOCIATION FREEWRITING: Write your topic or a keyword from your topic in the center of the page, and then write whatever comes to mind about it. If your assignment asks you to write a biography about an author, scientist, or painter, for instance, write the author's name in the center of the page. If you're writing about characters, use this technique for each character. If you're asked to write about a certain theory, write the keywords in the center and then write everything that comes to mind about it. This technique forces your knowledge and ideas onto the page and will give you a clear assessment of what you already know and what you do not. Don't worry about wording or organization. For now, just allow the ideas to express themselves; in other words, just get it all out.

The following example demonstrates Kim's timed, focused freewriting for analyzing the character Ophelia in Shakespeare's *Hamlet*.

OPHELIA

She is young and pretty, but she seems sad. Don't really know what to say about her. Is she having an affair with Hamlet? What's the deal with them? This play was hard to read! I'm stuck. Well, she kills herself, I think. But I don't think she does it just to get attention like that guy in our class said. I think she was trying to say something. Her dad seems nosy and in her business too much, and her brother also seems pushy and overbearing. Maybe she was tired of her dad and brother running her life. They always seemed to be telling her what to do, and then Hamlet tries to tell her what to do and then he dumps her. Maybe she felt isolated and abandoned by all the men in her life. It seems like she is maybe fifteen or sixteen, but she doesn't really have any say in her life; she has to do what everyone else tells her. Maybe that's what Shakespeare's trying to say, that she is controlled by everyone around her and the only way she could gain any power and control in her life was to end it? Yeah, maybe her suicide shows that she felt the only way she could be free was in death.

I guess that would go with the whole "something's rotten in the state of Denmark" thing that we talked about in class. She's part of the rottenness? Or maybe the way people treated her was the rotten part? I'm not sure, but I guess I need to get that quote about rotten stuff from the play. ... What does Ophelia do or say right before she commits suicide? Maybe I could use that as evidence. And am I sure she killed herself? I guess I need to check on that. Then I could try to prove that her suicide means something and has something to do with all the control they all had over her and somehow tie it to the whole rotten thing.

This writer has generated several ideas to explore for her paper:

1. How feeling subjugated affects Ophelia and leads to her death/ suicide
2. Ophelia's depiction as related to the theme of power that runs through the play
3. Why understanding Ophelia and her actions is important to understanding the play as a whole and the "rottenness" within it that many scholars address

BRAINSTORMING

Like freewriting, brainstorming is a method writers use to help them generate ideas. When brainstorming, you will write all the ideas that come to mind, just as you did in freewriting, but it will be a bit more organized than freewriting. Brainstorming often results in a list, chart, or map.

There are many, many different types of brainstorming. You will find on the following pages the most widely used brainstorming strategies and examples of each. Some of these techniques may work for you, but others may not. Keep in mind that some writers do not like or use brainstorming at all and prefer to begin simply with cold writing. Neither method is "right" or "wrong"; find what works well for you, and use it.

You'll notice that the brainstorming strategies are divided into two groups: *visual spatial* and *linear*.

Brainstorming is most effective when writers use both *linear* and *visual spatial* strategies. Why? Using different types of writing strategies engages different areas of the brain.

> *Employing both "right" and "left" brainstorming techniques engages **both** sides of the brain, which doubles your brainpower and leads to more insightful and creative expression.*

Since the left side of the brain controls writing and language, most beginning writers approach assignments only with left-brain strategies, such as writing sentences and paragraphs. Although this can be a successful strategy, engaging the right brain, too, will help elicit new, different ideas and ways of viewing the topic. The right brain controls spatial relationships and the imagination, so strategies such as the idea map or the Venn diagram can prove helpful for getting the right brain working on your topic. Indeed, many successful writers use *both* linear and visual spatial strategies when they approach an assignment so that they can tap into both right- and left-brained perspectives.

When you finish brainstorming, it may be helpful to see the end of this chapter for suggestions about how to use the ideas you solicited with your brainstorming techniques.

Like freewriting, brainstorming proves a helpful tool for writers at any point in the writing process. However, most writers find brainstorming especially helpful at the beginning of an assignment, when they need to get started and generate ideas.

It often helps to reread the prompt or assignment just before beginning your brainstorming session to ensure you have a firm grasp of what the assignment asks you to do.

You might choose to set a timer for your brainstorming session, depending on how well you work under pressure. If setting a specific end time seems to work well for you, then try that; if not, keep brainstorming until your page or diagram is full.

In the following sections, we will focus on these strategies:

LEFT BRAIN (LINEAR)
- Lists and Outlines
- Question and Answer
- Reporters' Questions
- Cubing

RIGHT BRAIN (VISUAL SPATIAL)
- Idea Map or Web
- Cluster
- T-chart
- Venn Diagram

You may not necessarily use all the ideas you elicit in your brainstorming, but at this point don't worry about restricting yourself to two or three main ideas. Just get your ideas stirring. In the beginning stages of a writing assignment, the more ideas you can generate, the better. Greater selection in the early stages of writing usually leads to greater creativity and depth of thought while brainstorming. Besides, having a long list of ideas from which you can choose is always better than scrambling for ideas later as you try to write the essay itself.

Don't feel like you have to try each of these brainstorming strategies for every single paper you write; the technique you use for each assignment is ultimately up to you, so feel free to experiment with different techniques. However, certain strategies do lend themselves to certain types of assignments, so you may find it helpful to see the "Idea Generation Strategies at a Glance" chart found later in this chapter, which indicates which strategies are recommended for the different types of writing assignments.

VISUAL-SPATIAL BRAINSTORMING STRATEGIES

Try the following right-brain strategies to engage your right hemisphere. If you are typically a left-brained person, these may be difficult at first, but using them will help strengthen your right hemisphere, which will improve your brain's ability to process and elicit information.

THE IDEA MAP OR WEB

The idea map (or idea web) remains among the most popular right-brain idea strategies because it works well to get ideas flowing and its structure makes converting your ideas to linear paragraphs a breeze. An idea map is exactly what it sounds like: a map that outlines your ideas. It nicely organizes your ideas on the page and reveals the connections between them.

To create one, write your topic in the center of the page and then write a major point in each of the three circles stemming from the center circle. Then write supporting information (such as evidence and explanations) in the smaller circles stemming from your point circles. You can draw as many or as few circles as you like, and don't worry if you do not fill in all the circles or if you need to add more circles. Just focus on getting your ideas onto the page.

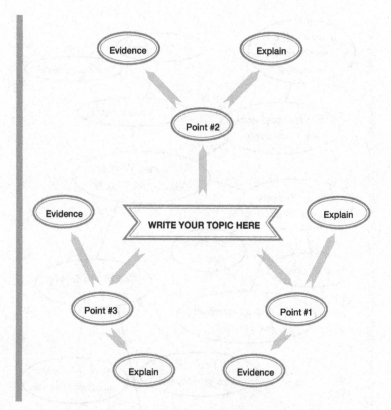

Once you've completed your map, sit back and look at it; you'll instantly see the type of information you have in abundance and what you lack. For example, do you have many points but little explanation and evidence, or is the reverse true? Either way, the idea map will clearly illustrate this information to you and will point to the areas that need further development. Take your strongest points from the idea map, and convert each into its own body paragraph.

This idea map, created by Russell, shows his brainstorming for an essay on wage increases for restaurant workers.

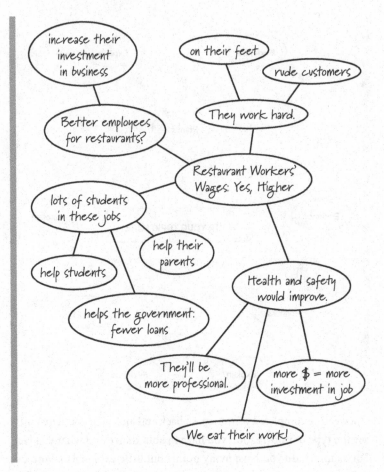

increase their investment in business

on their feet

rude customers

Better employees for restaurants?

They work hard.

Restaurant Workers' Wages: Yes, Higher

lots of students in these jobs

help their parents

help students

Health and safety would improve.

helps the government: fewer loans

They'll be more professional.

more $ = more investment in job

We eat their work!

T-CHART

Different writers use the T-chart differently, and its flexibility is one of its greatest assets for writers. The T-chart works well for comparison/contrast, pros and cons, or proponent/opponent assignments because it allows you to immediately see connections or differences between ideas or topics. It also identifies the topics or ideas you will need to flesh out more thoroughly. To create a T-chart, follow these steps:

1. Draw a Giant *T* on a piece of paper, or if you prefer to use a computer, create a table.

2. Write or type your first topic, text, character, or perspective on top of the column on the far left side of the page or screen; then write or type your second topic, text, character, or perspective on top of the second column, and repeat the process to add as many columns as you need.

TOPIC OR TEXT 1	TOPIC OR TEXT 2	TOPIC OR TEXT 3

3. Decide in which column you should begin, and then write everything that comes to mind about that topic, text, or character. You can time yourself if you like. Some writers set a timer for five to seven minutes, write in only one column the entire time, and then repeat the process for each column. Other writers simply write until they have filled each column or come up with a predetermined number of ideas.
4. Repeat this process in each of your columns.

This is a T-chart created by Jenny, who is writing on the topic of comparing and contrasting the depictions of two characters in similar familial roles in a film or television text.

PETER GRIFFIN (*FAMILY GUY*)	HOMER SIMPSON (*THE SIMPSONS*)
• Idiot • Fat • Lazy • Incompetent at job, goes through several jobs • Spends a lot of time at the bar • He is mean to his daughter, Meg, and seems like he could not care less about her. She is the family joke, and he encourages this. There are lots of episodes where he makes fun of her and calls her names. • He is mostly uninterested in the other kids unless they can do something for him; he spends more time with his friends than with his kids. • Peter treats Lois horribly; he is a terrible husband. I don't know if he ever actually cheated, but I think he would if he had the chance. I need to check on this. He and his friends check out other women all the time, which shows he sees marriage as a joke and doesn't take it seriously like Homer does.	• Idiot • Fat • Lazy • Incompetent at job, but keeps the same job for most of the show • Spends a lot of time at Moe's. (Does he spend as much time as Peter does? I need to check on that...) • He is nice to Lisa (most of the time, lol), encourages her a lot, and loves her; he wants the best for her. He sees her as the best thing he ever did and is a good father to her. • He fights a lot with Bart but has a definite connection and bond with him. There are lots of episodes about them doing things together. • I think Homer spends more time with his family than with his friends, definitely more than Peter spends with his family. • Homer is a good husband overall. He does *not* cheat on Marge, even when he has the chance. He and his friends don't really talk about and look at other women; do they? Need to check …

Jenny notes a couple of items she must verify within the texts; even though she is unsure of their accuracy, she has generated some excellent starting points. Even if all of her perceptions do not pan out, she will be in good shape because she has listed plenty of ideas here.

VENN DIAGRAM

The Venn diagram, like the T-chart, allows writers to easily compare and contrast ideas, topics, concepts, people, characters, time periods, paintings, and so forth. The Venn diagram helps writers examine the relationships between ideas so that the distinctions and/or overlaps within the concepts, patterns, or depictions become clear.

Like the T-chart, the Venn diagram will immediately reveal to you which topics you know the most (and least) about, and it will also clearly illustrate whether you feel the ideas or texts you compare have more differences or similarities. To create a Venn diagram, follow these steps:

1. Draw a large circle near the left margin of your page or document; extend the circle toward the middle of the page.
2. Draw another circle near the right margin of your page or document, but be sure its outer left side overlaps the outer right side of the first circle. In other words, the circles should connect to each other.
3. If you have three topics to compare or consider, draw a third circle on the bottom or top of the two original circles so that it, too, overlaps each of the two original circles. (Add one circle for each major idea you must examine, making sure each circle is connected to all others.)
4. Once the circles are drawn, write the first idea, topic, or perspective you must consider in the center of the first circle. Write this topic in bold or black, or underline it. Then repeat the process with each idea, topic, or perspective you will cover in your essay.
5. Start with whichever circle you like, and write everything that applies to that topic—*and only that topic*—within it. Don't write in the overlapping areas just yet.
6. Once each major circle is filled with ideas, move to the overlapping areas between the circles. These areas represent the shared characteristics, so now write in these spaces the commonalities of the topics or ideas. In other words, write what is true of *both* of the ideas or texts represented by the intertwined circles.

This process probably sounds complicated at first, but it's not too difficult once you see it in action.

This Venn diagram, created by Robin, compares and contrasts the depictions of father/daughter relationships in Shakespeare's *The Taming of the Shrew* and the modern-day movie *10 Things I Hate About You*.

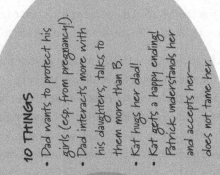

TAMING
- Dad is selfish & greedy
- Wants to sell them off
- Barely even talks to men who will marry his girls
- The whole "taming" with starvation and stuff
- Kate loses self

BOTH
- Overbearing dads
- No moms
- Suitors trying to help the girls fool their dad
- 2 daughters, older one is "the shrew," younger one is "perfect" but not really

10 THINGS
- Dad wants to protect his girls (esp. from pregnancy!)
- Dad interacts more with his daughters, talks to them more than B.
- Kat hugs her dad!
- Kat gets a happy ending! Patrick understands her and accepts her— does not tame her

LINEAR BRAINSTORMING STRATEGIES

Try the following left-brain linear brainstorming techniques to engage your left hemisphere. If you are typically a right-brained person, these may be difficult at first, but using them will strengthen your left hemisphere, which will improve your brain's ability to process and elicit information.

REPORTERS' QUESTIONS

Using reporters' questions ("Who?" "What?" "When?" "Where?" "How?" "Why?" and "So what?") to get ideas for a paper can be immensely helpful because doing so immediately reveals which areas of your paper need more information.

Each question may not apply to every assignment or text you are writing about, but the process reveals which questions you can immediately answer and which you cannot. For example, if you can easily answer "Who?" and "What?" but not "When?" or "Why?" you know you need to go back through your materials and see if you can or should figure out the answers to these questions. If not, that's fine, but the act of researching will build your knowledge of the topic and will lead you to other answers that you can include in your essay.

When answering reporters' questions, keep the following questions in mind:

- Who is involved in this topic? Who is affected? Who would care about it?
- What is/are the topic(s)? What are its implications? What are the outcomes and important points to consider?
- When will the issue be important? Is it contemporary and pressing? Timeless and classic?
- Where is the issue most important? Is a certain area or geographical location of particular importance?
- How will the information be presented in your essay? How will you organize your argument, data, or comparison? How will

you evaluate the sources you must include? How are you and your readers affected?

- Why is this issue important to consider? Why does it matter? Why would anyone want to read *your* opinion about it? Why are your ideas significant, unique, or of great value to readers?
- So what? Why should anyone give their interest and attention to this topic and your ideas on it?

The last question—"So what?"—is among the most important to address in an academic essay, and hopefully you noticed that it encompasses most, if not all, of the other questions. Your "So what?" answer is your smoking gun, so to speak; if the answer to this question is compelling, you've already set up your essay for success.

Read Russell's Reporters' Questions exercise below. Do you think he made an effort to elicit ideas on the topic?

Who?
Restaurant workers

What?
Pay and whether their pay should be raised

When?
??? Now, I guess.

Where?
In restaurants

Why?
???

So what?
No idea

These exercises only work if the writer truly puts their mind to coming up with ideas on the topic. It can be difficult to do sometimes, especially if the topic is one in which you have no interest. Clearly, Russell struggled with this particular topic.

If this happens to you, remember that you have options:

1. Switch the topic to one you find more interesting.
2. Ask for help; go to the instructor, to the TA, to your campus writing center, to a learning lab, or even to a friend or family member.

Russell opted for the second choice and decided to seek his professor's help. He wanted to do well in the class but just could not come up with many ideas on the topic. Below, you can see the comments the instructor made.

Who?
Restaurant workers

Good—you have identified a specific group, but which restaurant workers? Do you mean managers, CEOs, waiters, hostesses, and bartenders? Specify which workers you will address; the assignment calls for a discussion of tipped employees, so you will probably want to focus there.

What?
Pay and whether their pay should be raised

All you have done here is repeat the prompt. Take a stand: Yes or no? What is your stance? Why?

When?
??? Now, I guess.

"When" may or may not matter too much in your argument; if you want to take a historical perspective and compare wages of these employees now to another time period, it might be interesting or it might not. You'd have to look into this.

Where?
In restaurants

All restaurants in the world? The assignment calls for a discussion of U.S. tipped employees, so try being more specific.

Why?

???

Explain why you feel the wage should be raised or not. What is your evidence? Why do you think as you do?

So what?

No idea

Who is affected by this potential raise besides the employees? What is the impact of giving the raise—or of denying it? Why should readers care about this issue at all?

Here is the resulting page from Russell's next brainstorming session.

Who?

Servers, bartenders, and cooks because they're the ones who handle our food and drink directly. Also, people who eat in restaurants, so restaurant customers are a who, too ...

Also whoever decides whether they get the raise or not. Their managers or owners? The customers? Not sure ...

What?

Raise their pay

Their hourly pay is too low for all the work they do: $2.13 per hour is ridiculous.

When?

Now versus in the past.

A historical perspective might be good.

From Google: This comes from some federal law back in the day that said their pay should be half of the minimum wage. Because they get tips, they don't need the whole hourly minimum wage, but they should get half of it to make sure they can pay their bills and stuff. That makes sense. I think that's going to be my argument: Their wage now should be half of the minimum wage now, too. It was then, so why isn't it now?

Why doesn't it just automatically go up like minimum wage does? Has anyone tried to get it raised?

Where?
The United States. I wonder if maybe other countries or even different states have different policies on this, and if they do pay their tipped people more, are their restaurants better and safer somehow?

Why?
Why should we raise their pay?

I guess food safety is really the big thing. I think if we pay them more, they'll do a better job and work harder to make sure our food is safe. Maybe we could make them get certified in food safety or something as a condition of the pay raise?

So what?
I guess this is what I already said about the whole safety thing. I think this might be the best angle to get readers to care, especially if they are not working for tips. They might get mad and think it's going to cost them more, so I better talk about that.

LISTS AND OUTLINES
Making a list or outline of your topic or ideas can help generate more ideas, and it can also help you get organized.

The List
The list can often lead to the formation of the outline. Whether you use full sentences or just jot down ideas, the list can help you explore the

topic and your thinking on it. The list can also work as a sort of to-do command sheet for approaching the paper.

Some writers simply write or type their topic on a blank sheet of paper or on the screen and then type all the ideas that come to mind. (Don't worry about organizing yet.) Other writers like to break down the topic by paragraph and make a list for each. Still other writers come up with ideas first and then make a list from each idea. Try one or all of these methods to see what works best for you and your writing.

The Outline

An outline provides the writer with a clear trajectory, or a skeleton, of the paper's organization. The outline should indicate what each paragraph will prove (or even what each *sentence* will prove, depending on how detailed you wish to make the outline).

As with the list, the outline varies by writer. Some writers compose an overall outline of the paper's goals and points, while others outline each paragraph separately and in great detail, specifying (sentence by sentence) exactly what information will be covered.

In Russell's sample brainstorming below, he tried the listing brainstorming strategy while writing a persuasive essay about whether or not a specific group of tipped employees should be granted a federal hourly wage increase. To see how he used this brainstorming to write an essay, turn to chapter 2.

Raise the wages of restaurant workers:
- Restaurant workers work really hard and have to deal with the public.
- Their work can affect our health; we need to make sure our food is safe.
- More money for these people means better food quality and standards in restaurants. Quality costs.
- People enjoy eating out. It reduces stress, which probably leads to a calmer population, which may even reduce crime.

- Restaurant workers' service provides people a neutral space where they can meet and form associations with others, whether in business or personally.
- Not everyone tips, so they sometimes might miss out on money they have actually earned.
- Paying them more would help the economy because it would put more money in circulation.

Possible arguments against:

- Shouldn't these workers be clean and handle food properly anyway, without getting a raise?
- How will restaurants pay for this wage raise? Owners will fight this idea.
- They're not doctors or scientists working on our top diseases or problems, so why should they get more money?
- Couldn't people form associations somewhere else? What do the servers have to do with these associations?

My rebuttals:

- Restaurant workers should be clean and handle food properly, but better pay usually encourages professionalism.
- What kind of money are these restaurant owners making? If they are almost broke and can't afford to pay more, that's one thing, but it seems like they're doing pretty well. If they have tons of money, then why can't they pay their workers more than $2 per hour?
- It's true that restaurant workers are not performing brain surgery. But like I said, their work does affect the public's health. There are lots of people who aren't solving our great problems, and they make tons of money. Isn't food safety worth more than $2 an hour? I'm not saying they should be millionaires.

- Having someone wait on you in a neutral territory is important when forming associations with others. If someone's your enemy, you're not going to go to his house and have him wait on you. You need a neutral place run by neutral people.

QUESTION AND ANSWER (Q & A)

Try the following exercise either to help gather ideas or to further specify them. You can follow the recommended time limits (given within the parentheses) if you wish, or simply write until you are tired or out of ideas.

The key to this exercise is to be honest and avoid censoring your ideas. Answer as many or as few of the questions as you wish, but try to write or speak for at least fifteen minutes total.

1. Write or talk about your current essay overall. Specifically, answer the following question: What I am really trying to say in my paper? (seven minutes)
2. What is the primary evidence I examine in my paper? (five minutes)
3. Why do I think this evidence is significant? Why will my readers find this evidence significant? (five to seven minutes)
4. What is the first text's (essay, book, poem, short story, film, research study, painting, composition, etc.) primary message or theme? Why do I think this? (five to seven minutes)
5. What is the second text's (essay, poem, short story, film, research study, painting, composition, or short story, etc.) primary message or theme? Why do I think this? (five to seven minutes)
6. What are the biggest questions I still have about this essay? (five minutes)
7. What are my next steps for this paper (such as visiting my instructor during office hours, making an appointment with the writing center, rereading my class notes, or writing out a timeline for completion)? (five minutes)

ESSENTIAL WRITING SKILLS FOR COLLEGE & BEYOND

Once you answer these questions, you will have an excellent idea of which elements of the assignment you have mastered and which you have not. Question 1 addresses points; question 2 addresses illustrations; question 3 addresses explanations. You will learn more about each of these three crucial elements (Points, Illustrations, and Explanations, or "P.I.E.") in chapter 3.

Below is Kim's Q & A on the topic of analyzing the character Ophelia in Shakespeare's *Hamlet*.

1. What am I really trying to say in my paper?
What I'm trying to say is that I think Ophelia killed herself and that her suicide gives us an important message. Umm ... what is the message?? I think the message is something like she couldn't take the rottenness anymore or something like that. She felt so controlled by everyone else and so overwhelmed by all the horrible things that were everywhere around her, like murder and revenge and incest, that she just couldn't stand to live anymore. It literally drove her crazy. I think that is what I'm trying to say, that Ophelia killed herself to avoid the rottenness of Denmark.

2. What is the primary evidence I examine in my paper?
I'm looking at other scholars' ideas about Ophelia and what they think, especially about her death or suicide. I think I should find some other people who also think she committed suicide so I can show that other people agree with me. So far, lots of other people say this, too, but they think she did it for different reasons than I do. I'm not sure if that matters or not.

3. Why do I think this evidence is significant? Why will my readers find this evidence significant?
I have to include research to support my argument, so I have to have people who agree with me, but I was also

thinking about bringing in some people who don't agree and then talking about why I think they are wrong. I think readers will find this significant because it will show them why my argument actually makes more sense and presents more evidence than the opposing views.

4. What is the first text's (essay, book, poem, short story, film, research study, painting, composition, etc.) primary message or theme? Why do I think this?

I'm only using one text, *Hamlet*, and I think the main message is don't try to get revenge on people because it will just backfire and ruin your whole life and everyone else's life, too. People in the story went crazy, killed each other, and almost everyone dies. I think Ophelia's suicide really shows how terrible things got there just because Hamlet wanted revenge.

5. What is the second text's (essay, poem, short story, film, research study, painting, composition, or short story, etc.) primary message or theme? Why do I think this?

N.A. *(This question should raise a red flag for Kim; she writes that the question does not apply to her because she is only writing about one text,* Hamlet, *but she should double-check the prompt to be sure she is not required to write on more than one text.)*

6. What are the biggest questions I still have about this essay?

I'm worried that I'm not going to have enough to say and the paper won't be long enough. Maybe I should consider including info about the world in general at that time, specifically about how girls lived, to understand what it was like for someone like Ophelia? Can I do that? I guess I need to ask.

7. What do I still need to do?

I just realized I have not even started working on citing the sources. I need to do this ASAP! Ask Professor Brown how to cite that article I found online!

CUBING

Some writers use a cubing tool to help generate ideas. "Cubing" means considering your topic from six different perspectives. Just as a cubed dice has six sides, a cubed brainstorming session will result in six "sides" or approaches to your topic. Do your best to write about all six "sides" of the cube, but keep in mind that not every side will apply to all topics or assignments.

Take out a sheet of paper, or open a blank document on your computer. Take three to five minutes to write about your topic from each of the following six perspectives (give *each* perspective three to five minutes):

1. **COMPARE AND CONTRAST IT.** In what way(s) are the subject, texts, or ideas similar and/or different?
2. **ASSOCIATE IT.** Connect the material to something you care about, know, or understand.
3. **ANALYZE IT.** Break down the prompt into parts, and address the meaning of each part in relation to the whole.
4. **APPLY IT.** Apply to the "real" world; in other words, "So what? Who cares?"
5. **DESCRIBE IT.** How does the subject look, sound, taste, smell, or feel?
6. **ARGUE FOR AND AGAINST IT.** What are the pros and cons? Who agrees with you or not, and why?

If your writing prompt actually contains one of the above terms, you may want to spend additional time on that "side."

When you finish with all six sides, you will see which side seems most interesting or relevant. If one particular side was easy for you to consider and write about, this may be the perspective to focus on in your essay.

Below you will find the first four sides of Robin's cubing on her topic of comparing the depictions of fathers and daughters in *The Taming of the Shrew* and *Ten Things I Hate About You.*

1. COMPARE AND CONTRAST

SAME: The plot is basically the same: daughters having trouble with their fathers being too overbearing and having too much say in their lives. The father characters are sort of the same, but they're also different. Both dads want the best for their daughters, but Baptista seems more distant and also more interested in marrying them off than really making sure they get the best guy. The girls' characters are pretty much the same. Bianca is like the perfect one who is "daddy's little girl," and Kat is the outcast who is seen as a troublemaker, but Mr. Stratford actually tells Kat at the end of the movie that he's proud of her for being like she is, for being so tough and for not just settling for any guy who comes along. I guess that would be a difference because Baptista never says anything like that to Katherina. He seems to want to change her so he can be rid of her; he doesn't accept her for who she is.

DIFFERENT: Mr. Stratford is much more protective of his daughters than Baptista is. Baptista seems like he is more interested in getting rid of them than in protecting them. I mean, he lets some guy he met five minutes before marry his oldest daughter! He doesn't even know Petruchio, but he lets him talk to Katherina alone and then even agrees to let him marry her! Mr. Stratford won't even let a guy take his girls to prom without meeting them first. I guess that's another difference: The girls in the play are dealing with marriage whereas the girls in the movie are dealing with dating.

2. ASSOCIATE

I really related to the film more than the play because of the way the dad is so protective and won't let Bianca date unless her sister does. I was the younger sister, too, and my dad often punished me for my sister's decisions, which is how Bianca feels her dad treats her. I liked how the film made Bianca more relatable and explained her behavior. She can't understand why her dad won't let her make her own decisions and trust her judgment. Just because Kat does or doesn't do something doesn't mean Bianca will. Not sure what else to say or how I could tie that into my essay ...

3. ANALYZE

This is the hard part for me. What parts should I look at? I guess I could look at how the girls' relationship with their father (is this the part?) relates to the play or film itself (is this the whole?) Without the conflict between the father and the daughters, there really wouldn't be a plot. The whole story revolves around the dads' interference in their lives, so maybe the meaning of the whole story is related to that, the power the father has over his daughter's lives. Is Shakespeare saying that's a good thing? Is the film saying that? I hope not! I think it's terrible. It's like the dads decide their fate or something.

4. APPLY

I guess the "real world" application would be why we still care about this story hundreds of years later. Does the remake show us anything about how much we've changed over time? Maybe I could talk about how the dad in the film seems to have a better relationship with the daughters and seems to see them as people instead of stuff to sell off or be rid of. Maybe this is why he has a better relationship with them.

IDEA-GENERATION STRATEGIES
AT A GLANCE

Although each of these strategies can help generate many different types of information depending on the writer and the assignment, the chart below indicates which strategies have proven the most helpful for eliciting the specific type of information indicated.

WHAT YOU NEED	TRY THESE STRATEGIES
Organization	Idea Map, Outline, Venn Diagram
Relationships Between Ideas	Idea Map or Cluster, Venn Diagram, T-chart, Cubing
Compare/Contrast	Freewriting, T-chart, Venn Diagram
Pro/Con	Freewriting, T-chart, Outline, Cubing
Ideas in General	All Freewriting and Brainstorming Strategies, especially Free Freewriting
Evidence	Q & A, Reporters' Questions, Cubing

BEYOND COLLEGE

Many jobs require employees to be able to compare and contrast different policies, ideas, candidates, or products, and your future employer may also expect you to be able to brainstorm and outline new ideas on the spot. The Venn diagram and the T-chart in particular are considered invaluable tools for idea generation in business, education, government, and economics.

HOW TO USE YOUR
BRAINSTORMING AND FREEWRITING

After you brainstorm and freewrite, you may face a difficult question: How can you turn the ideas on the page or screen into an actual essay? The answer depends on the writer.

Some writers begin composing the draft immediately after brainstorming and/or freewriting; they simply look at the page and see the structure of their essay, so they're ready to write. Other writers need more organization first, so they prefer to create a coding system, an outline, or another brainstorming session.

Regardless of your process, remember that you do *not* have to write the draft in a certain order; you don't need to write the introduction first, then the body paragraphs, and then the conclusion. If, while brainstorming, you get a flash of genius regarding the conclusion, go ahead and write it. Don't get bogged down with the order in which you "should" write. You can always go back and write the introduction later.

Don't forget that even after you begin writing your essay, if you get stuck, you can always go back to brainstorming and freewriting. Keep working on it and trying different techniques until you find one that works for you.

You will find on the following pages strategies writers use to turn idea-generation sessions into workable material for essays. However, don't feel as though you *must* complete these strategies. If you feel ready to compose the essay, then by all means move on to chapter 2. If you would like more help in organizing and structuring the ideas you have generated, then try one or both of the strategies to follow.

GROUPING AND LABELING

In this strategy, the writer labels each sentence or idea within her freewriting. This activity will help you see what elements of your paper (Points, Illustrations, or Explanations, also known as "P.I.E.") have taken form and which have not. For more information on "P.I.E.," see chapter 3. To use this strategy, follow these steps:

1. Read through your brainstorming or freewriting. Don't label anything yet; just read.

2. If you wrote your ideas by hand, get out a colored pen or pencil (use a different color than the one you used for brainstorming or freewriting); if you typed your ideas, open a new blank document.

3. Read through your ideas again. If you wrote out your ideas by hand, use the colored pen or pencil to circle each idea or piece of information you believe you can use in your paper. If you used the computer, copy and paste the "usable" information into the new document. You may want to begin by considering all of your ideas as "usable"; you can always cross them out or simply move them to a "trash heap" page later. Regardless of your decision, *don't delete any of your ideas!* Sometimes an idea or detail may not seem important, but you later realize you need it after all. If you wrote by hand, put the paper in a folder and hold onto it until you've completely finished the assignment. If you composed on the computer, use a "trash" page or document and name the file "Paper 1 Trash Page" or something similar. (Remember, you never know when these seemingly irrelevant ideas will later prove important or helpful to you.)

4. Go through and label each idea or piece of information so that you know its potential function in your paper.
   - Label major points by writing or typing a large *P* next to them.
   - Label evidence and examples by writing or typing a large *I* next to them.
   - Label information that explains points and evidence with a large *E*.

5. Count how many points you have, and then highlight each one and write or type it in large print onto a blank page or screen. Leave plenty of room underneath it, and space each point far enough away from the others to distinguish each one.

6. Decide where each illustration will go, and write or type that location underneath the appropriate point in smaller print or font. Do the same with all explanations.

Review your work; you should have several points listed, with evidence and explanations listed under each point. These will form the basis of your essay's paragraphs. If you only had one or two points, that's okay. More ideas will come to you as you write.

In the below example, Jenny has completed steps 1 through 4 of the Grouping/Labeling strategy, which she applied to her compare/contrast analysis of Peter Griffin and Homer Simpson.

Notice that her brainstorming has generated several points (P) she can explore, and with all the illustrations (I) she has listed, she probably will not have trouble defending these points. However, notice how few explanation (E) statements she has. Assuming she has correctly labeled her ideas, this exercise has revealed what elements of her paper she has begun writing already (P and I) and which she has not yet developed (E). She also noted a few items she was unsure about (those labeled with a question mark); as she writes the essay, she can decide whether this information is useful to her.

PETER GRIFFIN (FAMILY GUY)	HOMER SIMPSON (THE SIMPSONS)
• Idiot (?)	• Idiot (?)
• Fat (?)	• Fat (?)
• Lazy (?)	• Lazy(?)
• Incompetent at job, goes through several jobs (I)	• Incompetent at job, but keeps the same job for most of the show(I)
• Spends a lot of time at the bar (I)	• Spends a lot of time at Moe's (I). (Does he spend as much time as Peter does? I need to check on that.)
• He is mean to his daughter Meg and seems like he could not care less about her. She is the family joke, and he encourages this (P). There are lots of episodes where he makes fun of her and calls her names (I).	• He is nice to Lisa (most of the time, lol), encourages her a lot, and loves her; he wants the best for her (I). He sees her as the best thing he ever did and is a good father to her (P).

PETER GRIFFIN (FAMILY GUY)	HOMER SIMPSON (THE SIMPSONS)
• He is mostly uninterested in the other kids unless they can do something for him (P); he spends more time with his friends than with his kids (I). • Peter treats Lois horribly; he is a terrible husband (P). I don't know if he ever actually cheated, but I think he would if he had the chance. Need to check on this (I). He and his friends check out other women all the time, which shows he sees marriage as a joke and doesn't take it seriously like Homer does (E).	• He fights a lot with Bart but has a definite connection and bond with him (P). There are lots of episodes about them doing things together (I). • I think Homer spends more time with his family than with his friends, definitely more than Peter spends with his family (P). • Homer is a good husband overall (P). He does *not* cheat on Marge, even when he has the chance. He and his friends don't really talk about and look at other women; do they (I)? Need to check …

This example shows steps 5 and 6 of Jenny's Grouping/Labeling work. She has first listed her "P" statements and underneath copied her "I" and "E" statements. Notice she remained uncertain about the usefulness of some of her "I" statements, but she included them anyway. She can always delete this information later if she decides it proves irrelevant.

PETER

- He is mean to his daughter Meg and seems like he could not care less about her. She is the family joke, and he encourages this (P).
- Incompetent at job, goes through several jobs (I). (Not sure this "I" goes with this "P.")
- There are lots of episodes where he makes fun of her and calls her names (I).
- He is mostly uninterested in the other kids unless they can do something for him (P).
- He spends more time with his friends than with his kids (I).
- Peter treats Lois horribly; he is a terrible husband. (P)

- I don't know if he ever actually cheated, but I think he would if he had the chance. Need to check on this (I).
- He and his friends check out other women all the time, which shows he sees marriage as a joke and doesn't take it seriously like Homer does (E).

HOMER

- He sees Lisa as the best thing he ever did and is a good father to her (P).
- Incompetent at job, but keeps the same job for most of the show (I). (Not sure this "I" goes with this "P.")
- Spends a lot of time at Moe's (I). (Does he spend as much time as Peter does? I need to check on that.) (Not sure this "I" goes with this "P.")
- He is nice to Lisa (most of the time, lol), encourages her a lot, and loves her; he wants the best for her (I).
- He fights a lot with Bart but has a definite connection and bond with him (P).
- There are lots of episodes about them doing things together (I).
- I think Homer spends more time with his family than with his friends, definitely more than Peter spends with his family (P).
- Homer is a good husband overall (P).
- Homer does *not* cheat on Marge, even when he has the chance. He and his friends don't really talk about and look at other women; do they (I)? Need to check …

GETTING IT OUT: 7 STEPS TO DRAFTING

Now that you have generated ideas and worked to organize them, you can begin drafting your essay. Keep in mind these tips as you draft.

1. **YOU DON'T HAVE TO WRITE YOUR ESSAY "IN ORDER."** Don't feel you must rigidly stick to writing the introduction first, then the body paragraphs, and then the conclusion. Some writers compose their introduction last and their conclusion first, and others write the body paragraphs first and compose the introduction and conclusion paragraphs last. Experiment with writing different parts of the essay in different orders, and then do what works best for you.

2. **WRITE YOUR FIRST DRAFT AS RAPIDLY AS YOU CAN.** In writing the first draft of your essay, try to get as many ideas down on paper (or on the computer screen) as quickly as you can. Don't worry about spelling, grammar, punctuation, repetition, or irrelevance—just write. Don't pause to delete or cross anything out. You will have time to edit later; for now, let your ideas flow without any censorship.

3. **COMPOSE THE ESSAY USING MULTIPLE METHODS: TYPE AND HANDWRITE IT.** Each writer has a different relationship to their computer versus the classic pen-and-paper method. Even if you always type your essay from start to finish, try handwriting some of it or vice versa. Switching your method will switch your thinking and thus lead to new and different ideas and strategies. If you try switching methods and it doesn't work for you, you don't have to keep doing it—but at least give it a try.

4. **DON'T LET A BLOCK IN ONE SECTION STOP THE ENTIRE ESSAY'S COMPOSITION.** When you are writing your first draft, you will probably find that you don't have all of the material you need for a finished essay. For example, you may know that you need more evidence to support your points but cannot think of any. If you experience a block in a particular section, simply write yourself a bracketed note that details what you need and then move on. For example, your note may look something like this: "[INSERT

EXAMPLE HERE]." You can always add the evidence later, but for now you are free to move on to the next section or point.

5. **WRITE IN TIMED—AND UNTIMED—BLOCKS.** When composing, try writing without a time limit until you run out of ideas. Clear your schedule so you can sit as long as you need, and just allow the ideas to flow. The next time you write, do the reverse: Set a time period (ten minutes, for example), and write the entire time period without stopping. When the time limit expires, put the pen down and walk away.

6. **TALK IT OUT.** Discussing your ideas is one of the best strategies for composition. Most people do more talking than writing, so they feel more accustomed to explaining ideas aloud. If you begin to stutter or repeat yourself, it will probably be more obvious in speech than in writing. Plus, articulating your essay aloud forces you to clarify and succinctly convey your points and evidence. This strategy also helps you find new ways of wording and explaining your ideas. Whether you talk to your roommate, instructor, or even just yourself, talking about your work helps you become more direct about your current stance, and it often leads to newer, better ideas as well.

Ask the person you speak with to play devil's advocate; in other words, encourage them to find holes in your logic and consider perspectives, rebuttals, or questions you may not have yet considered. Addressing other people's criticisms and/or questions will strengthen and improve your thinking on the topic—and, of course, your writing on it.

7. **KNOW WHEN TO WALK AWAY.** Kenny Rogers was right. Knowing when to walk away is an invaluable skill, especially for a writer. You will almost certainly hit walls or blocks as you write your essays and other assignments in college, but if you learn when to keep going and when to walk away, you'll save yourself much time and aggravation.

Keep going when you feel you are onto something, when you're riding a wave of inspiration, or when you can feel it coming but it's not yet arrived. Sometimes the best ideas or inspirations come in the midst of working through a block.

Walk away when you can't seem to get it done no matter how hard you try. If you work and work and work and still aren't making any progress, it's time to walk away. Ironically, sometimes the best strategy for working on an essay is not working on it. So give yourself a break. Go outside. Get a cup of coffee. Go out with your friends. Watch an episode of your favorite show, take a nap, or read a book—just do what it takes to give yourself space from your work for *a while* (don't stay away too long!). When you feel ready, go back and try again, and hopefully your muse will show up and inspire you. I have found she always does—if you're patient ...

BEYOND THE CLASSROOM

Imagine you work for an environmental company, and your supervisor has asked you to create a presentation in which you must convince the audience that wind energy is a wise investment for their community. Just like in your academic papers, for your presentation you must achieve the following:

- Present a clear and convincing thesis
- Gain the audience's attention and trust so you can introduce the topic
- Outline your points, cite evidence to support them, and explain why the audience should agree with your perspective
- Leave the audience impressed with your final conclusions so that you persuade them to agree with your perspective and take the action you recommend

Remember that when you write essays for your college classes, you are essentially presenting your ideas, and if you apply the drafting tips you learned above, you will be able to create work that will impress and persuade your audience.

• PART II •
COMPOSING YOUR

ESSAY

CHAPTER 2

Your Ideas

The college essay requires students to develop their own ideas and also to address the ideas of other scholars. In this chapter we will focus on developing *your* ideas, but keep in mind that you will need to address the perspectives of other scholars as well. If you write with this overall understanding in mind, you will avoid making one or both of the two major mistakes beginning writers typically make in their college writing assignments:

1. **TOO MUCH OF "THEIR IDEAS":** Excessive summary of other scholars' work and ideas
2. **TOO MUCH OF "YOUR IDEAS":** Complete omission of other scholars' work and ideas

Neither of these approaches will lead to a high score on your essay. Remember, successful academic writing requires the inclusion of *both* your ideas and other scholars' ideas.

Exactly how much of "you" and how much of "them" should gain representation in your essay? Unfortunately, scholars do not universally agree upon a specific percentage or ratio of "their" ideas to "yours." This ratio will likely depend on the topic, the discipline, and even the professor. However, a good rule of thumb does exist: Unless your instructor states otherwise, your essay should consist primarily of *your* ideas, with other scholars' ideas cited as a foundation and support for your own.

If you imagine your entire essay as a pie chart, think of your ideas as being the larger "piece."

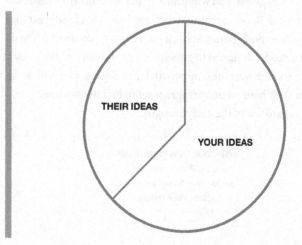

Because your ideas are so important, we will begin by addressing how to develop and polish them. Once you have a firm grasp of your own perspective, you'll be well equipped to address and evaluate other scholars' perspectives. If your instructor requires you to first complete research and then develop your ideas, or if you simply prefer this method, skip to chapter 4.

VISUALIZING THE ESSAY

Following this paragraph, you will find a visual breakdown of the essay so you can envision its overarching structure. This is not to suggest that you *must* have four body paragraphs in your essays; you do not. The diagram is just a model designed to give you an overall idea of the essay's structure. As you advance into upper-division classes, you will write longer papers with many more paragraphs, but luckily this same structure applies, regardless of the essay's length.

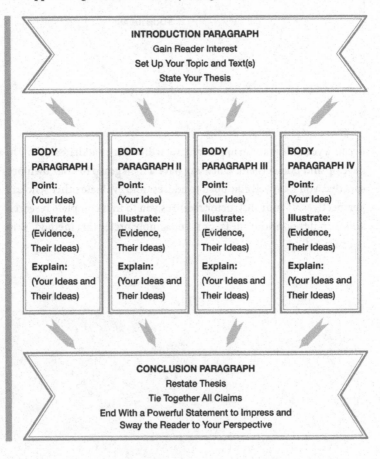

INTRODUCTION PARAGRAPH
Gain Reader Interest
Set Up Your Topic and Text(s)
State Your Thesis

BODY PARAGRAPH I
Point:
(Your Idea)
Illustrate:
(Evidence, Their Ideas)
Explain:
(Your Ideas and Their Ideas)

BODY PARAGRAPH II
Point:
(Your Idea)
Illustrate:
(Evidence, Their Ideas)
Explain:
(Your Ideas and Their Ideas)

BODY PARAGRAPH III
Point:
(Your Idea)
Illustrate:
(Evidence, Their Ideas)
Explain:
(Your Ideas and Their Ideas)

BODY PARAGRAPH IV
Point:
(Your Idea)
Illustrate:
(Evidence, Their Ideas)
Explain:
(Your Ideas and Their Ideas)

CONCLUSION PARAGRAPH
Restate Thesis
Tie Together All Claims
End With a Powerful Statement to Impress and
Sway the Reader to Your Perspective

NARROWING DOWN YOUR IDEAS

After you've completed brainstorming and/or freewriting, you will hopefully have some good ideas to mold into an essay. (If not, continue with the freewriting or brainstorming process.)

Now you must ensure the ideas you came up with are specific enough that you can write a thesis statement; in other words, the ideas should be so defined that readers can immediately determine *exactly* what your essay aims to discuss, prove, analyze, or examine.

PUT YOUR CARDS ON THE TABLE

When you present your point(s), be exact and defined in your language. In other words, put your cards on the table, so to speak. State exactly what you will attempt to prove in your essay. Avoid being vague or aloof in the attempt to inspire curiosity in the reader. This strategy may have worked in high school or middle school, but it will *not* impress academic readers. Professors do not see vagueness as an invitation to read more; they see it as a blaring neon sign that says the writer has no idea what they will discuss in the essay. Such vagueness will translate into a poor score.

Remember, academics do not sit with bated breath, excited to discover your ideas. Professors want the bottom line first and the proof and details later. If the bottom line is interesting, then they'll examine your proof to make sure it's solid. If the bottom line does not interest them, then they see no point in examining the evidence, and if they decide this is the case, it will probably translate into a failing score.

Think of your essay as akin to your hand in a poker game, and think of your thesis statement as the sentence that reveals that hand. Your thesis statement should answer this central question: What do you have in your hand?

Don't bluff. Academics can spot a bluffer quicker than a dog can spot its favorite bone. (Remember, your professors read hundreds of essays *each semester,* not to mention they were once students themselves ...). If you don't have a good hand, keep working on it until you do.

Read Robin's example statements below to see how she took vague, general ideas and molded them into specific, clearly defined ideas for her essay.

> In *10 Things I Hate About You* and *The Taming of the Shrew,* father/daughter relationships are depicted in both similar and different ways.

How well has Robin addressed the prompt? Can you discern what point each major body paragraph will address? If you think it's hard to tell, you're right. Robin doesn't present a claim but instead states an obvious fact. She needs to outline the specifics of her analysis: How do the depictions differ, or do they—and why are these depictions significant?

Here, Robin narrows her topic.

> In both *10 Things I Hate About You* and *The Taming of the Shrew,* the father figures have excessive control over their daughter's love lives; however, Mr. Stratford has much better intentions than Baptista does, which imparts an important understanding within both texts.

Robin now presents a claim statement with which she can argue, and she has further specified her argument. However, she still needs to be a bit more specific to ensure readers fully understand her thesis. For example, she needs to define "better intentions" and "an important understanding." These phrases are still too vague to allow us to follow her argument.

Here, Robin narrows her topic further.

> Both texts depict controlling father characters and show that the motivation behind this control determines the daughter's ultimate fate. Baptista's selfish motivation leads to a horrific ending for Kate, but Mr. Stratford's benevolent motivation leads to a happy ending for Kat.

Robin has now better defined her ideas on the topic, and we can discern the overall structure of her essay:

- **BODY PARAGRAPH 1:** Comparison of each text's "controlling father" characters
- **BODY PARAGRAPH 2:** Baptista's motivation and its connection to Kate's "horrific ending"
- **BODY PARAGRAPH 3:** Mr. Stratford's motivation and its connection to Kat's "happy ending"

BEYOND THE CLASSROOM

Most of us have sat in boring presentations or endured long-winded writing in which the speaker or writer rambled on and on and on—for several sentences, paragraphs, or pages—before finally stumbling onto their main point. This type of communication won't likely win you favor with your bosses, colleagues, or benefactors. Therefore, it is crucial to learn how to narrow down your ideas so you can present them clearly and succinctly when given the opportunity.

In fact, many employers encourage or even require their employees to develop an "elevator speech" for their department, division, program, or product. The pitch is so named because it should last no longer than the average elevator ride (about one minute). It requires the speaker to succinctly and powerfully convey to others the most important points or attributes of what they do, make, sell, or offer—all in less than a minute.

Practice this skill of narrowing down your ideas now, and later you can impress your boss and clients with your verbal acuity.

THESIS STATEMENTS

The thesis statement is among the most important sentences in an academic essay; in fact, having a strong thesis is crucial to writing a strong essay.

> The thesis statement asserts the essay's main idea and purpose; the thesis immediately reveals to readers the essay's organization and expresses concisely what, exactly, the writer will discuss and prove.

THE THREE LAWS OF THE THESIS STATEMENT

1. The thesis statement outlines the essay's purpose and presents the essay's argument.
2. The thesis statement is *one* declarative sentence that is clear, specific, and arguable.
3. The thesis statement's argument matches the ideas presented within the body paragraphs.

THESIS STATEMENTS AT A GLANCE

THE THESIS STATEMENT *SHOULD*:

- Present an *arguable* claim
- Outline the essay's structure
- Clearly connect to the topic and prompt of the assignment
- Appear as the last sentence of the introduction paragraph
- Contain a "how" and/or "why" element
- Interest and engage readers

THE THESIS STATEMENT SHOULD *NOT*:

- Merely present a question
- Contain vague, unclear phrasing such as *many, some, very, really, kind of, a lot, there are, there is,*

certain way, *today, today's world, society, you, I,* and so on (See the "Banned Words and Phrases" section in chapter 8 for an in-depth discussion on these words and phrases.)
- Force the reader to guess what the paper will prove or discuss
- Include confusing language
- Present a fact or definition

If you begin to compose the body of your essay and you do not yet know what your thesis is, don't panic. The thesis statement will likely change and grow as you compose. Don't be afraid to alter or even completely change your thesis to reflect your new ideas and body paragraphs. However, once you've determined your position, *be sure your thesis statement reflects the arguments advanced in the body paragraphs.*

EXAMPLES
Read Kim's sample thesis statement below.

> Different scholars see and interpret Ophelia's death in many different ways, and in this essay, I am going to discuss these ways and why they are important for readers to understand.

This thesis statement is weak. It presents a vague answer that fails to outline either the argument or structure of the essay. It also tells us little about her perspective. What will Kim argue? What *is* her view of Ophelia's death? As readers, we have no idea. It sounds as though Kim has no ideas of her own and is simply going to tell us about others' ideas.

Instead of merely summarizing what *others* have written about Ophelia's death, Kim should address what she believes and outline that interpretation for us.

Never write, "In this essay, I will …." What is the point of announcing "In this essay"? Readers know the work is an essay; there is no need to say so. Nor do you need to make a declaration of "I *will* discuss … ." Readers understand that a writer will discuss information, so there is no need to announce this fact.

Don't tell the reader you *will* discuss a topic; just discuss it. In other words, instead of talking about discussing the topic, *actually discuss it*. You can do this by deleting the phrase "In this essay, I will" and then stating your point. If you don't yet have a point, reference the brainstorming and freewriting sessions completed earlier in the writing process.

For example, in her brainstorming session Kim wrote the following.

> Maybe that's what Shakespeare's trying to say through Ophelia, that she is controlled by everyone around her and the only way she could gain power and control of her life was by ending it. Maybe her suicide shows that she felt the only way she could be free was in death.

This is an interesting idea and much more specific than "other scholars see her death in different ways." This idea about control and its connection to her death could be developed further as an argument for the essay. For example, here is Kim's first revision.

> **Ophelia kills herself because she is controlled and rejected by everyone around her.**

The revised version shows improvement; the second half contains a claim. However, the phrase "everyone around her" is still too vague.

In the final revision, Kim rewrites this phrase to further specify.

> **By connecting Ophelia's suicide both to Polonius's control of her and Hamlet's rejection of her, *Hamlet* illustrates the**

> "rottenness" that young women like Ophelia experienced in Denmark: a dark confinement that could be escaped only through death.

Let's look at a different example from Russell.

> Anyone who argues restaurant workers' salaries should *not* be raised is an idiot.

Russell's thesis statement violates the bond between the reader and the writer because it offers an insult rather than a point. Never insult a group of people when attempting to persuade, for you can never truly know whether your reader is a part of the group you insulted. Attempting to hide behind insulting language rather than presenting facts and evidence will not impress or sway an academic audience.

Instead, Russell should present and set up his argument about *why* restaurant workers should earn higher wages. For this attempt, he re-reads his freewriting and realizes that he feels these workers deserve higher salaries because of the value of their work to our society. He writes the following revision.

> Restaurant workers deserve higher salaries because the work they do is important and affects us all.

This improved version of his thesis statement contains a claim with which we could argue. However, the sentence does not give us an idea of the essay's structure, and the ideas presented are still too vague. He needs to elicit more ideas, so he tries the Reporters' Questions brainstorming activity (see chapter 1) and writes out the following questions.

> **HOW?** *How* does the work of restaurant workers "affect us all"?
>
> **WHY?** *Why*, exactly, is the work they perform so important?
>
> **WHAT?** *What* type of monetary increase am I proposing?

WHO? *Who* deserves the raise? Should all restaurant workers earn more money or only the upper-level restaurant managers? Only food servers and cooks?

SO WHAT? Why would anyone care about this issue, especially those who do not work in restaurants?

Russell's final revision offers readers a clearly defined thesis statement with which we could reasonably argue. We can immediately tell what major points the paper will prove, and Russell has successfully presented us with an outline of the paper's structure.

Restaurant servers, bartenders, and cooks deserve at least a 25 percent increase in their current hourly wage because they ensure the safety and quality of public food and drink in restaurants and they provide a valuable service to our society: They allow diners to relax and enjoy camaraderie with others through shared bonding over food and drink.

CHECKLIST: REVISING THESIS STATEMENTS

Writing a detailed thesis statement is by no means easy; it takes time, patience, and practice. Few people expect beginning baseball players to hit home runs each time they step up to bat, and similarly, few professors expect beginning students to write a perfect thesis statement. However, the more you practice, the better you will become at writing them—and this expertise will not only earn you higher scores, but it will save you time and frustration as your writing assignments become more complex.

If you worry your thesis might not achieve all that it should, use the following checklist to help you revise it.

- ❑ The thesis statement references key terms from the essay's topic.
- ❑ The thesis statement outlines the essay's claims and primary position(s) on the topic.
- ❑ The thesis statement is arguable; it is not a statement of fact (in other words, reasonable people could offer conflicting opinions on the ideas presented).
- ❑ The thesis statement contains no vague terminology, such as "lots of reasons," "many similarities," or "I will explain in this essay ..." If so, replace these words with more specific terms. (For example, replace "lots of reasons" with the specific reasons you will discuss, and simply remove "I will.")
- ❑ The thesis reflects the organization of the essay and gives the reader an overall trajectory of the paper.
- ❑ The thesis statement is the last sentence in the introduction paragraph.
- ❑ The arguments stated in the thesis match the actual arguments of the body paragraphs.

CHAPTER 3

Breaking Down the Essay

COMPOSING THE BODY PARAGRAPHS: EASY AS P.I.E.

Most students have likely heard their English, art, or philosophy instructors say that there is no "right" or "wrong" interpretation in a persuasive or analytical essay. Students then wonder how instructors grade these papers if no "right" or "wrong" answers exist. The distinction in rhetorical analyses is not a matter of right or wrong but rather one of *convincing* versus *unconvincing*.

Building effective body paragraphs is absolutely crucial to writing a successful—convincing—argumentative essay.

A convincing, interesting body paragraph contains:

- A clear tie to the paper's thesis and to the paper prompt
- Topic sentences that state clearly what the body paragraph will prove
- Specific textual evidence to support each claim
- Clear explanations that tie together the claim and evidence to support the thesis

Think of writing the paragraphs as being easy as P.I.E.

Point
Illustrate
Explain

Each body paragraph should clearly state the Point: the purpose or claim of the paragraph, i.e. what the paragraph will discuss and prove.

Each body paragraph should contain myriad Illustrations: examples, quotes, evidence, and proof that demonstrate, support, and illustrate the point.

The writer must then clearly and effectively Explain the significance of all examples, quotes, evidence, and proof to ensure readers understand the importance of each.

VISUALIZING THE BODY PARAGRAPHS

As you compose the body paragraphs, consider the proportions of the component "slices," so to speak. How many sentences should be devoted to the point? To the illustrations? To the explanations? Different assignments and topics will differ in how many sentences each component will need. No set formula dictates, for example, that each body paragraph should have one point sentence with five illustration (evidence) statements and three explanation sentences. However, most of the body paragraph's information should work to explain and defend the point.

Your point sentence(s) will take up the smallest portion, while the illustrations (evidence) and explanations will occupy most of each body paragraph's space.

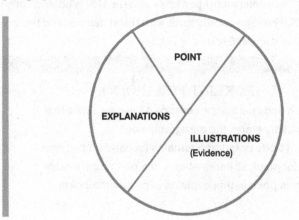

Let's now take a closer look at the three elements of body paragraphs.

POINT

- The *claim or position* the paragraph seeks to prove
- Stated immediately in a topic sentence (usually the first or second sentence of the body paragraph)
- Clearly addresses and answers the prompt
- Only *one* per body paragraph
- All information in the body paragraph should clearly tie to this *one* major point

FACT VS. POINT

A fact is not arguable because we can prove it. For example, the sentence "Some corporations in the United States do not pay taxes," is a fact, not a claim. We could check IRS or company tax records to verify this information. Use facts as *evidence,* not as points.

A point is a claim, an argument, or a statement of opinion. A point statement presents an idea with which we could argue. It is not a statement that can necessarily be proven as true or false but rather as having credibility or not.

For example, the statement "Corporations that do business with United States consumers must pay taxes into the U.S. economy," presents a *point*. Not everyone would agree with this statement, and there is no way to prove it absolutely true or not.

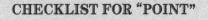

CHECKLIST FOR "POINT"

❏ Each body paragraph contains a topic sentence that explicitly states the paragraph's point.

❏ Each body paragraph remains focused on this one major point; all information in the paragraph relates to this point (either explains or proves the point).

- ❏ Each body paragraph's point reflects the argument outlined in the thesis statement.
- ❏ The order of the body paragraphs matches the order listed in the thesis.

EXAMPLES

Read Kim's first point statement. Does she present a claim?

> Ophelia shows up to Gertrude's castle acting "importunate" and "distracted," singing songs and then saying "good night" four times right before readers learn she is dead.

This statement presents a fact, not a claim. We can verify in the text whether or not this writer presents an accurate overview of Ophelia's final words and actions. Therefore, Kim has given herself nothing to argue. She needs to tell us *the significance* of this information; in other words, what is her point about Ophelia's final actions and words?

Now consider Kim's revision:

> Ophelia's cryptic final words clearly foreshadow her death and illustrate her plan to commit suicide.

The statement now presents a claim; readers could argue with this perspective. Now Kim must defend and explain the claim.

In the second example, another student, Russell, presents his first point statement. Is it a claim or a fact?

> Restaurant workers, such as servers and bartenders, are among the only workers within the entire workforce in the United States who have not been included in minimum-wage increases; in fact, their hourly wages have not been increased by federal law since 1991.

This statement also presents a fact, not a claim. We can verify with the Department of Labor that these particular workers' hourly wages have not increased in the time span indicated. Although this statement might work well as an illustration for a claim, it is not itself a claim statement. So far, Russell has not stated an *argument*.

Consider his revision:

> **If restaurant diners in the United States want to maintain clean, safe, and relaxing facilities in which to dine, they must support a federal minimum-wage increase for the servers, cooks, and bartenders who handle their food and drink.**

The statement now presents a claim; readers could argue with this perspective. Russell must now defend this claim with explanations and textual evidence to illustrate for readers *why* this increase in wage is so crucial and *how* this wage affects food quality and safety in restaurants as the statement indicates.

ILLUSTRATE

The "I" section of your body paragraphs provides your readers with evidence to support the essay's thesis (your overall argument), so be sure to spend ample time ensuring you have strong, convincing, and relevant evidence to support each and every point.

Citing evidence often sounds like a difficult, tedious process to many students, but remember that your ultimate goal is simply to support your point. The "I" section explains to readers why they should consider your perspective as valid. In other words, write your illustrations to answer this question: *Why should anyone believe your point?*

What information counts as "illustration" in academia depends on the assignment and the instructor. Read your assignment carefully to see if the instructor outlined the specific types of evidence you must include (such as research study results, quotes from in-class texts or notes, or specific authors or types of references you must cite). If so, be sure to follow these instructions closely; if not, ask the professor what types of evidence you can include. A philosophy instructor may allow you to include personal experience as an "illustration" in your essay, but an English or history professor probably won't.

Types of evidence to consider for your "I" section include:

- Quotes
- Examples
- Statistics
- Research findings
- Interviews
- Expert testimony or opinion
- Analogies
- Surveys

Remember to check with your instructor to ensure the evidence you cite is appropriate for the assignment. Once you determine the types of evidence to include, follow the three-step process outlined below:

1. **SELECT THE ILLUSTRATIONS.**
   - Be highly selective. Include *only* quotes and information that support and illustrate your point. Do *not* quote just to quote.
   - Cite only evidence from academic, scholarly sources (see chapter 4).
2. **SET UP THE ILLUSTRATIONS.**
   - Don't quote-bomb the reader. Set up and explain all quotes.
   - Assume that readers don't understand the quote's importance; explain it.
3. **CITE THE ILLUSTRATIONS.**
   - Always give proper credit to the texts you reference so you don't risk plagiarism charges (see chapter 10 for more on plagiarism).
   - Cite the information in your essay (in the paragraph) *and* at the end of your essay (in a Works Cited or References page).

QUOTING VS. PARAPHRASING

Many students struggle with understanding when to offer a direct quote from a text and when to simply paraphrase the author's meaning. Understanding the difference can help you illustrate your points effectively.

A quote is a direct, exact, identical, word-for-word restatement of material from another text or source.

A paraphrase is an indirect (*not* exact, identical, or word-for-word) restatement of material from a source. It is a summary of the text written in your own words.

Direct quotes offer powerful illustrations to present to your readers, but be careful you do not overquote. Readers expect most of *your* work to be *yours*, not a mere regurgitation of someone else's. Use quotations to build, support, and illustrate your point, but use them sparingly. Don't bury your reader beneath a heap of quotations.

When You Should Quote

From a fictional text (such as a short story, play, or novel):

- Important or precise dialogue, thoughts, or stage directions
- The narrator or speaker's specific commentary

From a nonfiction text (such as an essay, book, or journal article):

- Eloquent or impassioned language (such as expert testimony)
- Definitions or well-worded explanations

When You Should Paraphrase

From a fictional text:

- When referring to a specific event in a text
- When offering a summation of lengthy information, such as an entire passage or an overall synopsis of the plot or setting

From a nonfiction text:

- When the original information is too complex or lengthy to quote all of it

- When the exact language may not be appropriate or clear for your point(s)

EXAMPLES

Step 1: Select a Quote

Kim hopes to support her point that Ophelia's final words foreshadow her suicide. Read her illustration choice below; do you think she effectively selected an illustration to support her point?

"I hope all will be well. We must be patient, but I cannot choose but weep to think they would lay him i' the cold ground. My brother shall know of it. And so I thank you for your good counsel. Come, my coach! Good night, ladies, good night, sweet ladies, good night, good night."

Kim's choice of quote is not as effective as it could be. Though she uses Ophelia's precise language, which will offer strong support for her point, Kim does not need to use *all* of the quoted dialogue she cites. She should include only the specific portion of the dialogue that will illustrate her point. Unless she plans to address every word or phrase within the long quote, she needs to pare it down to only the essential elements she will discuss.

Consider Kim's revision:

> "Come, my coach! Good night, ladies, good night, sweet
> ladies, good night, good night."

Kim can now effectively address the shorter quote and explain why it proves her point.

Step 2: Set up the Illustration

Now that Kim has selected her illustration, she must set it up within her essay's paragraph. She must lead readers to the quote so they are prepared for it and do not feel as though she quote-bombed them. A writer "quote-bombs" when she simply drops a quote into a paragraph and does not properly set it up or comment upon it. Quote bombs disorient readers and leave them feeling confused about the writer's choice to switch from his own words to someone else's without signaling this change.

Read Kim's set-up sentences and quote inclusion below; see if you feel she has set up her illustration well.

> Ophelia's cryptic final words clearly foreshadow her death
> and illustrate her plan to commit suicide. Although some
> readers might be shocked when they read of Ophelia's
> death, the text does prepare readers for it. Ophelia her-
> self alludes to her suicide plan with the last words she ut-
> ters in the play. She says, "Come, my coach! Good night,
> ladies, good night, sweet ladies, good night, good night."

Kim plans to use the selected quote to argue that it 1) foreshadows Ophelia's death and 2) points to Ophelia's allusion to her suicide plan. Therefore, it is important to set up these points before offering the quote. This information gives readers a better understanding of why she offers this quote and sets up her late discussion of why she finds it so significant.

Kim will still need to explain *why* she feels the quote illustrates her point, but this information falls under the "E" (Explain) portion of the paragraph, which we will discuss on the following pages.

Notice that Kim has not yet cited the quote. This information is crucial; she must offer a reference to show the source from which she retrieved the quote.

Step 3: Cite the Illustration

As you will learn in chapter 7, writers must cite sources in two ways:

- In text (parenthetical)
- Works Cited (or References) page

In this particular case, quoting from a Shakespearean play within the body of the text, Kim must cite the play's abbreviation, act, scene, and lines.

> **She says, "Come, my coach! Good night, ladies, good night, sweet ladies, good night, good night!" (*Ham* IV.v.71-73).**

Kim must also include a Works Cited page at the end of her essay; this page contains a listing of all references she included in her text. To view examples and learn more about citing sources, see chapter 7. For more detailed questions on how to cite specific text, consult the appropriate writing manual for your discipline (MLA, APA, or Chicago style). If you are unsure which manual you must use, ask your instructor or librarian.

EXPLAIN

- Tie together the Point and its Illustration.
- Ensure your body paragraph clearly answers the question "So what?" in relation to the prompt.

Never assume readers understand the importance of your illustrations. If you do make this assumption, you will risk two situations that could prove devastating to your scores:

1. Readers will misunderstand or misconstrue your meaning.
2. Readers will assume you do not know how to cite evidence, and thus they will discount you as a writer with sloppy work that cannot be trusted.

> *The explanation section of your essay addresses **why** you included the evidence presented and **how** it illustrates your point.*

Use the following key explanation words to clarify these connections between your points and your evidence.

TO ADD	Also, and, further, furthermore, too, moreover, in addition to
TO GIVE AN EXAMPLE	For example, for instance, consider as an example, to demonstrate, to illustrate, in this case
TO COMPARE/CONTRAST	Whereas, but, yet, conversely, as opposed to, rather, on the other hand, however, nevertheless, less, more, greater, worse, better, neither, nor, both, and, more likely, less likely, despite, in spite of
TO PROVE	In fact, because, for, since, clearly, thus, indeed, by, as, makes clear, illustrates, demonstrates, exhibits, makes evident
TO SHOW EXCEPTION	Although, though, yet, still, however, nevertheless, in spite of, despite
TO CONNECT	Thus, clearly, in fact, indeed, of course, specifically, in particular

CHECKLIST FOR "EXPLAIN"

- ❏ The essay includes transition words that help cue readers to the connections between my ideas and my evidence.
- ❏ I fully explain the significance of each quote or paraphrase.
- ❏ I address and answer the question "So what?" in each paragraph so readers understand my ideas and their importance.

EXAMPLE

Consider Kim's sample list below, containing the three P.I.E. elements.

(P): Ophelia's cryptic final words clearly illustrate her plan to commit suicide.

(I): "Come, my coach! Good night, ladies, good night, sweet ladies, good night, good night."

(E): The "coach" is a reference to suicide.

Her repeating the phrase "good night" FOUR times shows readers she is planning to go away permanently, so her drowning was not an accident but a planned suicide.

She says "good night" rather than "good-bye" to foreshadow where she's going.

Now read her entire paragraph to see how she put the three elements together. The "E" (Explanation) words are bolded so you can easily recognize and consider them.

Ophelia's cryptic final words clearly foreshadow her death and illustrate her plan to commit suicide. **Although** some readers might be shocked when they read of Ophelia's death, the text does prepare readers for it. Ophelia herself alludes to her suicide plan with the last words she utters in the play. She says, "Come, my coach! Good night, ladies, good night, sweet ladies, good night, good night" (IV.v.71-73). Her call for a "coach" **exhibits** Ophelia's call for her own death; **because** she calls for it herself, she **shows** us she is planning it herself, **clearly** a planned suicide and not an accidental drowning. The "coach" is a metaphor for suicide; it is the vehicle she will use to get to her "good night," in other words, her death. The phrase "good night" comes right after her calling for the coach **to illustrate the connection between** the coach and the "good night." **In**

**fact, she repeats "good night" four times to demonstrate
to readers that she is not leaving temporarily but permanently.** Her specific phrasing matters, too; she says "good
night" **rather than** "good-bye" **to make evident** that it is
the night that she sees as good, so (like Hamlet in Act
II) Ophelia's words **show that she sees** death as a nice,
peaceful place to go.

Kim has indeed followed the structure of P.I.E.; she has provided an argument, listed evidence, and tied this evidence to her point.

INTRODUCTION AND CONCLUSION PARAGRAPHS

Strong essays contain both introduction and conclusion paragraphs. Effective opening and concluding paragraphs create the credibility and interest academic writers expect. Just as the body of the essay will certainly influence graders, so, too, will the introduction and conclusion paragraphs. Write these paragraphs well, and you will undoubtedly win points with your grader.

A STRONG, INVITING OPENING PARAGRAPH

When you browse for books in a bookstore, secondhand shop, or library, how do you decide whether to purchase or check out the book? Although different readers have different selection processes, most people decide whether they are interested in a book based on the first few paragraphs— or even the first few sentences or words of the book.

We often use this criterion for evaluating films and television shows, too; if a program does not gain our interest immediately, we change the channel or dismiss it as uninteresting and/or unworthy of our valuable time and attention. Remember this fact when writing your introduction.

You might think of the introduction paragraph as akin to the entrance of a home; it should invite readers to enter. An appealing introduction paragraph will set up and be indicative of the brilliant ideas present within the essay. If academic readers can't understand your argument by the end of the first paragraph, they won't want to read any further, so work hard to ensure you gain your reader's interest with your opening words. This is not easy to do, but spending time on your introduction will prove a smart and worthwhile investment— especially at the beginning of the semester. First impressions are hard to overcome, so associate your name and work with quality from the very beginning, and this association will likely stay with you for the rest of the semester.

AN IMPRESSIVE CLOSING

The conclusion paragraph influences readers' perceptions of the entire essay, especially when you are writing for grades. The final statement(s) of your paper will likely be the last one(s) the grader reads before assigning the essay a grade, so you will want these statements to impress the reader and convince them of the value and merit of your work. If the entire essay demonstrates a well-polished, interesting, and informative discussion but the conclusion paragraph proves sloppy, lazy, and/or incomplete, readers will walk away from the work feeling disappointed or disoriented, and such feelings are detrimental to your grade. Be sure to tie up all loose ends and connect each of your major ideas to give the reader the big picture of your topic and perspective.

It might help you to consider your essay as a puzzle that you—the writer—put together for the reader to view. The conclusion paragraph represents the last piece of that puzzle, and without this crucial piece, your reader will not be able to fully see the picture or scene you've created with your essay. The conclusion allows you to tie together each of the points from your body paragraph and explain in detail the larger "So what?" of your essay and the perspective it offers.

After reading the conclusion paragraph, the reader should be able to step back from your essay and see its picture. Be sure to remind the reader of each of the key pieces of the "puzzle" in the conclusion paragraph so she feels all of the important pieces are intact, all the gaps filled.

WHAT IS THE FORMULA FOR THE INTRODUCTION AND CONCLUSION PARAGRAPHS?

There is no set formula for "correctly" writing either the introduction or the conclusion paragraph. However, you can think of both paragraphs as having shapes like a triangle. The introduction begins with broad information and then slowly narrows down the topic until it reaches a point. The point represents the most specific sentence in the introduction—your thesis. The conclusion paragraph does the reverse:

It begins with the specific information argued in your essay and then broadens to include societal implications and calls to action.

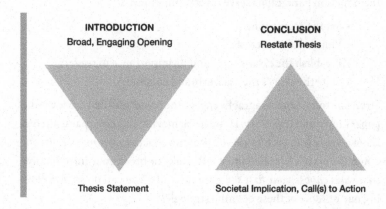

INTRODUCTION	CONCLUSION
Broad, Engaging Opening	Restate Thesis
Thesis Statement	Societal Implication, Call(s) to Action

On the following pages, we will explore both introduction and conclusion paragraphs in more detail.

INTRODUCTION PARAGRAPHS

Introduction paragraphs serve several functions:

- Set the essay's tone
- Pique reader interest
- Establish the essay's topic and its importance to readers
- State the essay's thesis clearly and concisely

Strong introduction paragraphs engage the reader and make evident the paper's topic and trajectory. However, achieving this clarity and interest is not an easy feat. So, how do you write an effective opening paragraph? Often the essay's first statement will make or break your introduction, so *always choose your first sentence carefully*. You can do so by following one or more of these opening strategies:

- Ask a thought-provoking question.
- Offer a shocking or unbelievable fact.
- Cite an interesting, provocative quote.
- Present a problem.
- Describe a compelling image.
- Provide a definition.

All of these strategies can work well in an essay, but they certainly do not guarantee an effective opening. The key to creating a compelling first sentence is simple: Ensure its *relevance* to your topic and ideas, and do not be afraid to point out this relevance to readers.

Quotes, questions, definitions, or statistics provide great openings for essays, but remember to always explain their significance. Answer the question, "Why have I included this information?" but don't assume your readers understand why. Tell them. For example, citing an interesting quote from Darwin, Shakespeare, Einstein, or another famous thinker may seem impressive, but if that quote bears no clear relation to your topic, readers will immediately be confused or annoyed—*not* impressed. Ensure that you clearly tie any information you offer directly to your topic.

Never offer readers a dictionary definition, whether in the introduction paragraph or anywhere within an essay, without commentary or explanation. Always follow up on definitions; otherwise, your work will seem lazy and elementary. Any student can slap a word's definition into their essay, and in fact this method has been so misused that many instructors have banned it. Only include a definition if you find it interesting, compelling, or lacking. Then, explicitly address this interest and/or lack.

EXAMPLE

Consider Jenny's sample introduction paragraph comparing and contrasting the depictions of Homer and Peter as husbands/fathers in their respective shows.

> Is *The Simpsons* or *Family Guy* a greater television program? Lots of critics have put these shows down for as long as they've been on the air. Both Peter and Homer are inadequate as leaders and providers for their families, but Homer is overall a good and caring husband and father, whereas Peter is a selfish and uncaring one.

As it stands, this introduction paragraph would unfortunately fail to impress an academic audience. I've outlined its specific strengths and weaknesses below.

> **"Is *The Simpsons* or *Family Guy* a greater television program?"**
> **YES:** The writer opens with a question and immediately points to the texts she will examine.
> **NO:** The opening question confuses readers and muddies the topic. Asking the reader his or her opinion about the greatness (or lack thereof) of these programs seems irrelevant to the topic of comparing and contrasting the

characters' depictions. Instead, Jenny should introduce the importance of these characters, specifically within their roles as husbands and fathers.

"Lots of critics have put these shows down as long as they've been on the air."
YES: It might be interesting to address the critical commentary of the programs.
NO: Raising the issue of critical commentary only works if Jenny ties this commentary to her topic. What is the connection between the critical reception of the program and the depictions of the husband/father characters? Jenny should also formalize her tone here; the language she uses is a bit too informal for an academic audience. (For example, she should spell out the contraction *they've* and rephrase "lots of critics" and "put these shows down.")

"Both Peter and Homer are inadequate as leaders and providers for their families, but Homer is overall a good and caring husband and father, whereas Peter is a selfish and uncaring one."
YES: This statement, presumably the thesis, addresses the prompt and presents an interesting claim with which readers could argue.
NO: Jenny's jarring jump to the thesis from a vague statement about critical commentary will confuse readers; she should set up the texts and characters to lead the reader to her thesis.

CONCLUSION PARAGRAPHS

Conclusion paragraphs give writers one last chance to convey the importance of their argument to readers (and, of course, to convince graders that the essay deserves a high score). Conclusions do not merely restate the thesis, and most professors detest the phrase "In conclusion ...".

> *When writing a conclusion paragraph, consider this central question: How does your essay help readers to better understand the topic?*

The tasks your conclusion fulfills will vary according to your subject, audience, and objectives; generally, though, conclusions fulfill a rhetorical purpose—in other words, they persuade your readers to do something: to take action on an issue, to change a policy, to make an observation, or to understand or see a topic differently. You can achieve this by following one or more of the closing strategies listed here:

- Offer a stronger, more emphatic version of the thesis.
- Tie together all claims and evidence to illustrate the validity of your thesis.
- Close with a thought-provoking question to spur readers to think further on the topic.
- Cite an interesting, provocative quote.
- Point out the areas within the topic that need further investigation.
- Present a solution to the problem discussed in the essay.

As with introduction paragraphs, these concluding strategies only work well if they are relevant to your essay as a whole.

Set up your final statement(s), especially quotes and questions; you will not have further space to explain them, and you do not want your reader to walk away from the essay confused. Make sure to be specific in calls to action so readers will know exactly which actions you recommend.

You shouldn't assume readers will understand the importance of the quote or question offered in your conclusion. Be careful not to over-simplify a large and complex issue or problem or introduce new points or material.

EXAMPLE

Consider Russell's sample conclusion paragraph on the topic of wage structures in the contemporary United States:

> Nobody wants to work hard all day on his feet, dealing with loud and rude customers and then not make any money. How can we expect quality food and service from these people for only $8 per hour, including tips? This wage amounts to barely $.75 above the minimum wage, while their high and mighty bosses get millions in bonuses! Sure, bosses should make more than their workers, but not this much more. It is imperative that we all get involved and do what we can to make sure the servers and bartenders who handle our food and drink receive a respectful living wage for the work they do.

As it stands, this concluding paragraph would unfortunately fail to impress an academic audience. I've outlined the conclusion's strengths and weaknesses below.

> **"Nobody wants to work hard all day on his feet ..."**
> **YES:** Russell attempts to restate an important point stated within the essay.
> **NO:** The restatement of the point must be more direct. If the point is that high-quality workers will leave the restaurant industry for work that garners more respect and higher wages, then Russell should say so. Also, he needs to formalize the language and avoid generalizations (such as "nobody wants").

"How can we expect quality food and service from these people ..."

YES: This sentence raises an interesting question and reminds readers of important evidence stated in the essay (the specific wages of these workers).

NO: Again, Russell should formalize the language; the reference to restaurant workers as "these people" seems insulting. If his goal is to humanize these workers so readers will empathize with them, he must use more inclusive language.

"This wage amounts to barely $.75 above the minimum wage ..."

YES: These sentences remind the reader of points addressed in the essay.

NO: Again, Russell must formalize his tone and specify the language. The point that "bosses should make more" remains undefined. How much more does Russell advocate? How much is too much? Also, he should avoid the name-calling ("high and mighty bosses") and tie this statement to the thesis. How or why does this enormous gap between the boss and the workers' salaries threaten diners' enjoyment and safety in restaurants?

"It is imperative that we all get involved and do what we can ..."

YES: This sentence is a call to action.

NO: This call to action is vague and thus ineffective. What, exactly, can readers do about this issue? Should they boycott restaurants? If so, which ones? Perhaps they should write their state or national senators to raise the state minimum wage for tipped employees. Russell should offer specific courses of action for this strategy to achieve its effect.

INTRODUCTION AND CONCLUSION WRAP-UP

- **DON'T FEEL OBLIGATED TO WRITE THE INTRODUCTION PARAGRAPH FIRST AND THE CONCLUSION PARAGRAPH LAST.** Many writers work on their conclusion long before they finish the paper, and some writers compose the introduction last.
- **WRITING A STRONG INTRODUCTION PARAGRAPH FREES YOU TO USE THE SPACE WITHIN THE BODY PARAGRAPHS TO *DEFEND AND EXPLAIN YOUR ARGUMENT.*** Without a strong introduction, writers must use the body paragraphs to set up the argument, leaving little space for proving and explaining it. This mistake often costs the writer two letter grades.
- **BUILDING AN ESSAY IS, IN MANY WAYS, LIKE CONSTRUCTING A BUILDING.** Beginning with a shaky, insubstantial foundation in your introduction paragraph will lead to a flimsy, substandard building, and the builder (you, the writer) will have to deal with the headaches that accompany poor construction.

View as an investment the time and energy spent constructing a strong foundation in the introduction paragraph. Once you construct this foundation, you can then safely discuss and explore increasingly complex issues within the body paragraphs and remain confident that your work will stand up to any grader's scrutiny.

Remember the four main purposes of introduction paragraphs:

- Set the essay's tone.
- Pique reader interest.
- Establish the essay's topic and its importance to readers.
- State the essay's thesis clearly and concisely.

Remember the three main purposes of conclusion paragraphs:

- Restate the thesis to remind readers of the essay's overall purpose.

- Tie together all the essay's information to make it cohesive and coherent.
- End powerfully to illustrate the validity and importance of the essay's perspective.

Use the following checklists to ensure your introduction and conclusion paragraphs fulfill their purposes.

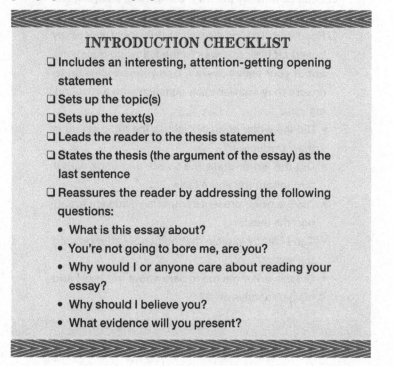

INTRODUCTION CHECKLIST

- ❑ Includes an interesting, attention-getting opening statement
- ❑ Sets up the topic(s)
- ❑ Sets up the text(s)
- ❑ Leads the reader to the thesis statement
- ❑ States the thesis (the argument of the essay) as the last sentence
- ❑ Reassures the reader by addressing the following questions:
  - What is this essay about?
  - You're not going to bore me, are you?
  - Why would I or anyone care about reading your essay?
  - Why should I believe you?
  - What evidence will you present?

CONCLUSION CHECKLIST

❑ Restates the thesis

❑ Does *not* introduce new points or ideas

❑ Ties together all points and evidence to illustrate the credibility of the essay's perspective

❑ Ends powerfully (offers a compelling image, question, quote, or call to action)

❑ Readers will gauge the successfulness of your essay based on their answers to the following questions about your essay overall. Use your conclusion to ensure they answer each question with a resounding yes.

- Did the writer actually discuss the topic set up in the introduction?
- Did the writer state the thesis and stick with it throughout the entire essay?
- Did the writer present compelling evidence to support the thesis?
- Can I clearly explain that point now after reading the essay?
- Did the writer get me to care about this topic and his perspective on it?

CHAPTER 4

Their Ideas

WHAT IS RESEARCH?

At the beginning of this book we addressed the three crucial components of the college essay:

1. Your Ideas
2. Their Ideas
3. The Connections or Intersections of Your Ideas and Their Ideas

We have addressed how to develop and present your own ideas; now we will move on to finding, understanding, and including "their" ideas within your paper. Finding and understanding their ideas requires research.

In academia, to "research" is to deeply investigate the facts, conversations, and evidentiary support on a topic or text. When you research, you find and read articles, books, or other publications on your chosen topic or text. Then you must incorporate this information into your paper so that it supports and enhances your own ideas.

WHY CONDUCT RESEARCH?

You may wonder why conducting research is valuable. Aside from the obvious reason (because instructors assign research papers and you want to receive a good grade on your papers), to answer this question, consider for a moment why you enrolled in college.

Probably, you attend college classes for one of two reasons:

1. To increase your own knowledge and understanding of the world
2. To get a stable, well-paying, and rewarding career

Knowing how to conduct research is essential to accomplishing either of these goals. You cannot possibly extend your own knowledge without conducting research, and most well-paying and rewarding careers require some form of research. So if you look at research as a tool for helping you achieve your life goals (rather than a tiresome, pointless task you're being forced to do), it will be more enjoyable for you—and you will be more successful at it as well. You have to do it, so you might as well enjoy it!

WHO ARE "THEY"?

Think of finding your sources as finding "them," the people whose ideas you will address in your essay. However, before you can find valid sources, you must understand whom your instructor expects you to cite.

Who "they" are depends on the course for which you must write a research paper. In a biology class, "they" will likely be other scientists, doctors, or researchers. In an English class, "they" will likely be writers, poets, or literary critics. In an art history class, "they" may be artists, painters, sculptors, or art critics.

However, if you follow one simple rule, you will likely be safe:

Cite only the work of scholars.

What makes a person a "scholar"? A scholar is a specialist, an expert, a distinguished professional, or an academic *with credentials* to prove her knowledge, expertise, and experience. Scholarly sources always provide these credentials. Look at the book's sleeve or jacket for information on the writer's background, or flip or scroll to the end of an article to read about the author's professional experience or academic affiliation.

The form in which information is presented also provides you a clue about whether it is scholarly or not. In academia, you will find that essentially two source types are safely agreed upon as "scholarly": books and journal articles.

This is not to say that every book ever published is considered scholarly; clearly, this is not true. Celebrities write gossip-bearing tell-all books, and athletes regularly employ ghostwriters to record and share their exploits. You probably already recognize these example as *popular* texts, not academic ones.

However, if you can answer yes to the question below, then you likely have a safe, scholarly source to use for your essay:

Can you find the book or article in a college or university library?

Academic librarians take ordering library materials very seriously, and rarely will you find nonscholarly sources on the shelf. Any popular sources that you do find will be clearly labeled as "popular" or "leisure" reading. The same goes for accessing materials through an academic library's online services. If your library pays for a subscription to a database in which you find an article, you can probably cite it in your essay.

SCHOLARLY VS. POPULAR

This chart details examples of scholarly and popular sources.

	SCHOLARLY	POPULAR
SOURCE	Journal articles, books (depending on source), newspaper articles (depending on source)	Most online articles, most magazines, most newspapers, most (if not all) blogs
AUTHOR	Proven experts in the field, with credentials and the basis of expertise on the subject clearly cited (such as degrees or equivalent professional experience in the field). Examples: professors, doctors, economists, or scientists	Self-proclaimed "experts" or "gurus," such as columnists, bloggers, or celebrities; so-called credentials come from popular acclaim, based on appearances in film or popular television program(s).
PURPOSE/ MOTIVATION OF PUBLICA- TION	To evaluate knowledge within a given field, theory, or topic; to criticize or challenge a position or theory; to share research findings; to present documented discoveries with other professionals and experts	To entertain, frighten, advertise to, or thrill readers—but above all to make profit and/ or deliver the reader/customer to advertisers (who probably paid for the publication)
QUALITY	Use of highly polished scholarly or technical language: free of grammar, spelling, or punctuation errors; includes proper citation and use of other credible academic sources; readers usually need knowledge of the field and its vocabulary to understand the material	Slang and informal, simple language is employed. May contain grammar, spelling, and/or punctuation errors (though not necessarily); does not properly use and/or cite credible sources; likely cites other popular sources as "research" or "proof"

	SCHOLARLY	POPULAR
AUDIENCE	Specialized, limited audience; academics, such as professors and students; experts in the field, such as doctors, scientists, or other researchers	Wide audience, typically with mass appeal and created specifically for mass consumption and the general public
EVALUATION PROCESS	Extensive, lengthy peer review process conducted by several experts within the field of discussion to ensure the article or book's validity, accuracy, relevance, and timeliness	No extensive evaluation process; rarely, if ever, evaluated by anyone other than the writer and perhaps one editor
TIMELINESS	Includes clear date and place of publication, does not present itself as "latest up-to-the-minute" news or information, usually includes *both* historical basis *and* current research	Often presented as "breaking news," stresses modernity or latest fad, publication copyright date may or may not be included
ADVERTISING	Any ads that appear are small in size and do not play a major role spatially or thematically in the publication. The material is not presented by "sponsors" who may influence or promote a certain position, perspective, or argument.	Many and/or large advertisements are included in the publication. The author or entire publication may be paid for by "sponsors" who seek press coverage for their business or product and thus heavily influence the material and conclusions presented.

THE ACADEMIC CONVERSATION: THE GREAT DEBATE

Think of academic writing as akin to entering an ongoing conversation in which different speakers have already entered and exited and new ones—like you— enter. This conversation is not a casual one; it is more accurate to think of it as a debate, and in fact it is often referred to as "The Great Debate." Different scholars within different fields are, of course, debating different topics, and you as a student get to enter these debates.

As you can imagine, to enter this debate intelligently, you need to have an idea of what the speakers have (or have not) already said; if you don't take the time to research this information, academics simply will not listen to you or your ideas.

Think of your essay as now including not only your ideas but also their (other scholars') ideas, too. We focused in the prior chapters on developing *your* ideas; now, we will focus on finding and understanding *their* ideas so you can connect them to yours. Think of it this way: At this point of the writing process, your essay will include two major elements:

> *What **you** think and what **they** think*

Of course, professors do not expect you to know every conversation that has ever occurred between any and all academics on every topic in every field. It would be impossible for anyone to gain this much knowledge, so don't feel pressured to find every idea, theory, point, or conversation within your topic.

> *Focus on becoming familiar with **the key scholars'** names, works, and ideas within the topic on which you are writing.*

Most professors will provide you with a list of the key scholars in the field or discipline about which you must write. If you do not receive a list, consider asking for one. If the professor expects *you* to discover who these people are as part of the assignment, don't panic. This is easier than it sounds.

WHERE DO I START?

To learn what scholars have (or have not) said in the larger academic conversation, you must conduct research. You can start by asking the following questions:

1. What is the *field* I am researching?

   For example: molecular biology, Renaissance theater, twentieth-century American economic systems, nineteenth-century architecture, etc.

2. What is the *specific topic* within the field that I must research?

   For example: gender in Renaissance theater, inequities in twentieth-century American economic systems, etc.

3. Who are the *top scholars* within this field or topic?

   For example: Northrup Frye in literary criticism, Marshall McLuhan in media studies, Judith Butler in gender theory, Jack Zipes in fairy tales, Jackson Katz in men's studies, and so on.

RESEARCH: THE STAGES AND STEPS

Conducting research can be a stressful, confusing experience for many students. It can feel overwhelming to find sources, read them, quote them, and then cite them. This is indeed a lot of work to accomplish, but never fear. It's a lot less overwhelming when you break down the assignment into manageable pieces.

To get started, follow the steps listed below—in order—and you will write a strong, thorough research paper that may even prove enjoyable, rather than stressful.

Essentially the research process involves three stages, with seven steps total:

STAGE 1: PRE-RESEARCH

1. Determine your position or perspective on the research issue.
2. Prepare research questions and keyword lists.

STAGE 2: RESEARCH

3. Find sources.
4. Evaluate and understand these sources.
5. Select appropriate quotes and evidence from these sources.

STAGE 3: POST-RESEARCH

6. Incorporate the sources into your work.
7. Cite your sources using appropriate style (MLA or APA, etc.).

As you can see from the list of steps, a "research" assignment actually includes steps both before and after the actual researching. Remember, complete each step *one at a time*, to make the entire process easier—and less stressful.

We will go over each of these steps in the next three chapters. If you have never completed a major research project, I recommend you read the chapters in order; however, if you have written several research essays before, it may be more beneficial for you to flip forward to the areas in which you need the most help.

→ CHAPTER 5 ←

Pre-Research

Imagine a world-class runner in the precious few minutes before she competes in an Olympic event. She is probably stretching her body in preparation for the race. Or how about a world-renowned singer approximately an hour before a concert that thousands of people will attend? He is probably warming up his voice and mentally preparing for his performance. These two people have something important in common: They have a key event in front of them that they must perform well in to achieve the success they desire, and if they are wise, *they prepare for it.*

Conducting research similarly requires preparation. Many students don't realize this truth, so they make the mistake of getting the research assignment, heading straight to the library, and trying to research cold. Although everyone has different processes and this headfirst strategy might work for a few students, most students (probably 95 percent) benefit from prep work completed *before* beginning research.

To prepare for researching, you will need to *pre-research.*

1. Determine your position on the research issue or topic.
2. Prepare research questions.
3. Write out keyword lists.

Don't worry; these steps won't cost you a lot of time. In fact, *they will ultimately save you time.* Any energy expended on pre-research serves as a wise investment that will later bring you many returns. It will reduce your frustration level and help you focus on *writing*, rather than stressing over researching. This focus translates into greater confidence, which in turn translates into better grades.

Since we already covered how to determine your position in chapters 1 and 2, in this section we will focus on developing research questions and keyword lists. However, if you need help determining your position on the research topic, see chapter 2 on writing a strong thesis.

GETTING ORGANIZED

TIP 1: BE SURE YOU UNDERSTAND THE ASSIGNMENT.

Ask yourself the following questions. Write down or type the answers, and keep up with this sheet of paper or Word doc.

- What perspective will I take on the topic? (Sum up your perspective in a sentence or two).
- What types of sources must I find? Scholarly books *and* journals? How many of each type, or does it matter?
- How many sources or quotes must I include? Does the assignment dictate a desired word count or required research percentage? (For example, 50 percent of the paper must be research or "their" ideas.)
- How current must the research be?
- Does the instructor require me to cite opposing viewpoints, or may I cite only evidence that supports my perspective?
- Are there any specific sources that I must cite (such as specific books or articles mentioned in class)?

TIP 2: VISIT YOUR PROFESSOR—BEFORE YOU START RESEARCHING.

Share your ideas on the topic with your instructor before you waste any time researching. Imagine how frustrated you will be if you spend days researching a perspective only to have your professor tell you it was an invalid or uninteresting one. Invest a few minutes in a conversation with your instructor to ensure you're on the right track. You might even ask for suggestions on sources (these suggestions could save you *hours* at the library!).

TIP 3: CREATE A BINDER FOR THE RESEARCH PROJECT.

Everyone approaches organization a bit differently. I'm suggesting one method, but feel free to modify it to best suit your own project.

- Go out and buy a three-ring binder, dividers, and sticky tab markers.
- Put the dividers into the binder, and then organize them as follows:
  - In front of the dividers, place a printed copy of the assignment, with the prompt highlighted.
  - Label the first divider "My Work," and place in this section all of your own work (such as freewriting, brainstorming, etc.).
  - Label the second divider "To Use," and insert all the articles or book titles of sources you think you will use.
  - Label the third divider "To Be Read," and insert all articles or citations of sources you need to look over more carefully.
  - Label the fourth divider "Discards," and insert all articles or citations of sources you don't think are going to work. *Don't just throw them in the recycle bin!* You may change your mind about their value later ...

THE RESEARCH QUESTION(S)

If your assignment does not present to you a specific question or questions to answer, rewrite it so that it gives you a central question or two that you must address. Be as specific as possible when writing your question(s); this specificity will help immensely when you begin to research. It may mean the difference between thumbing through hundreds of hits versus dozens.

> *Break down the research prompt into manageable parts, and then turn each part into a question you must answer. Then **write your paper to answer the question(s).***

Consider the following example.

PROMPT: Compare/contrast the depictions of father/daughter relationships in *The Taming of the Shrew* and *10 Things I Hate About You*, and explain the significance of these depictions within the overall text. Specifically, address which text, if either, presents a better, more comprehensive view of the father character in terms of his relationship with and to his daughters. Cite research to support your contentions.

Break down the prompt into manageable parts.

This prompt, for example, contains essentially three parts:

FIRST PART: Compare/contrast the depictions of father/daughter relationships in *The Taming of the Shrew* and *10 Things I Hate About You*.

SECOND PART: Address which text, if either, presents a better, more comprehensive view of the father character in terms of his relationship with and to his daughters.

THIRD PART: Cite research to support your contentions.

Write a question for each part.

FIRST QUESTION: What are the major similarities and differences between how the play depicts father/daughter relationships versus how the film does?

SECOND QUESTION: Does either text present a better (more comprehensive view) of the father character in terms of his relationship with his daughters?

THIRD QUESTION: What do other scholars say about the father/daughter relationship in each text?

The writer now has three questions to answer in her paper. Notice she used her own language when rewriting the questions; she wrote them so she could understand them but kept the professor's meaning intact.

Consider Russell's example; it demonstrates how he turned his essay prompt into three research questions.

PROMPT: Considering our unit on contemporary wage structures in the United States, select a specific group of employees addressed in the textbook or in class and argue either in favor of or against a mandated federal hourly wage increase for this particular group of workers. All essays must include both citation of supporting evidence and refutation of counter evidence.

BREAKING DOWN:

FIRST QUESTION: What group of employees addressed in the textbook or in class will I select?
ANSWER: Tipped employees in restaurants, specifically cooks, bartenders, and servers

SECOND QUESTION: Am I going to argue in favor of or against a wage increase for these workers?
ANSWER: I am arguing in favor of a wage increase for them.

ESSENTIAL WRITING SKILLS FOR COLLEGE & BEYOND

THIRD QUESTION: What is my evidence to support and my counterevidence to refute?

ANSWER:

Support

- They haven't had a wage increase in more than twenty years, even though most other workers have, and this is not fair.
- Restaurants are making tons of money, aren't they? Why aren't they sharing the profits with the employees?
- There's already legislation in Congress right now; some senators are asking for this wage increase, so lots of people are already talking about this.
- Raising their wages will help us have healthier and safer food and better service because workers will be happier.
- Maybe a wage increase will help the economy because this sector of the workforce will have more money to spend. They'll get off welfare and other government programs. (I need to check on this.)

Counter

- It will be too expensive for restaurants, and they'll charge customers more, which will cause people to eat out less.
- Other people, like teachers, are doing more important work, and *they* should get the raise, not just some food servers.

Russell has done an excellent job of covering most aspects of the prompt. The amount of time and space he spent writing out his evidence (both supporting and counterevidence) will help him immensely later. However, he must remember to *refute the counterevidence* in his essay; otherwise, readers might misunderstand his stance on the issue.

CREATING YOUR KEYWORD LIST

Keywords are important words or phrases within a topic or thesis. Smart researchers know that creating a list of these words *before* beginning a research project greatly expedites the search. To create this list, follow the steps below.

STEP 1: Underline the key terms from your writing prompt *and* thesis statement. Pay particular attention to:

- The texts' titles and authors
- Specific themes, characters, or other elements you will address

Write down these keywords, or type them onto a blank page.

STEP 2: Write as many synonyms as you can for each word (use a thesaurus or dictionary, if need be), and don't be afraid to cater the synonyms to what you already know about the texts.

Write out as many forms of the keyword(s) as possible. For example, if you are writing about images of masculinity in advertising, you might write: *men, males, boys, masculine, masculinity, maleness, manliness, machismo, advertisements, advertising, advertise, and ads.*

STEP 3: Choose the best keywords from the list, and combine them to create a representative phrasing of your topic. *Balance* is the key here. Your phrasing should be specific enough to make your search manageable but not so specific that you find no results.

- **TOO VAGUE:** Hundreds, possibly thousands, of results
- **TOO SPECIFIC:** Few, possibly zero results
- **JUST RIGHT:** Ample results but not an overwhelming amount

In this example, the student must write on depictions of gender in contemporary American popular culture texts. His keyword lists are below.

- **TOO VAGUE:**
    - Gender and contemporary America
    - Men and American popular culture

- Masculinity and television
- **TOO SPECIFIC:**
  - Violent male gender roles in contemporary American print couture clothing ads in *Men's Quarterly* magazine in 2014
  - Machismo in contemporary American action films of 2014 starring Miles Marner
- **JUST RIGHT:**
  - Violent male gender roles in American action films
  - Violent masculinity and American magazine advertisements
  - Masculinity and American television sitcoms

EXAMPLE

Below you will find Robin's paper prompt, which she reviewed before starting her research. She highlighted important words within it (shown here in bold) and then used this information to create her keyword list, which you will find below as well.

PROMPT: Compare/contrast the depictions of **father/ daughter relationships** in Shakespeare's *The Taming of the Shrew* and Gil Junger's film *10 Things I Hate About You,* and explain the significance of these depictions within the overall text. Specifically, address which text, if either, presents a better, more comprehensive view of **the father character** in terms of his **relationship with and to his daughters.** Cite research to support your contentions.

MY THESIS: Both texts depict **controlling father characters** and show that the motivation behind this control determines the **daughter's** ultimate fate; **Baptista's selfish motivation** leads to a **horrific ending** for **Kate,** but **Mr. Stratford's benevolent motivation** leads to a **happy ending** for **Kat.**

KEYWORDS	SYNONYMS
father/daughter relationships	father/daughter bond? Parent/child bond?
Shakespeare	
Gil Junger	
The Taming of the Shrew	
10 Things I Hate About You	
relationship with his daughters	connection? affiliation? value?
controlling father characters	dominating, domineering, overbearing
Baptista	
selfish motivation	self-serving, egotistical, greedy
horrific ending	appalling, shocking, sad
Kate	
Stratford	
benevolent motivation	well meaning, kind, caring, protective
happy ending	fate, destiny, outcome
Kat	

PHRASES FOR SEARCHING:

- *The Taming of the Shrew*
- Father/daughter relationships in Shakespeare
- *The Taming of the Shrew* and *10 Things I Hate About You*
- Overbearing fathers in films
- Controlling fathers in Shakespeare
- Father's motivation and daughter fate

Robin now has a list of possible phrases from which she can choose when she begins researching.

CHAPTER 6

Research

If you read nothing else about researching at the college level, read this:

Do **NOT** rely exclusively on Google or other Internet search engines for your research sources. Using these searches as an *initial* helper in getting ideas is great because you can assess the general conversation and learn the key ideas and thinkers in the field. However, expecting Google will deliver *all* the sources for your essay will almost certainly ensure both frustration and failure. Why? Most Google sources are popular, rather than scholarly. (We'll discuss these types of sources in further detail on pages 109–10).

For now, simply remember this:

DO NOT rely solely on Google searches to find your sources for academic writing.

You may be wondering, then, where else will you find sources?

> Conduct research through your **university or college library**, too—
> not just the public library or Google.

Whether you need scholarly books, newspaper articles, journal articles, or historic archives, you'll find them through an academic library. (Public libraries may be able to help you, but most of these libraries are geared to *public* taste and entertainment, rather than academic research and documentation.)

Once you arrive at your college or university's library, whether in person or online, you'll find vast, sometimes overwhelming, resources. It therefore helps to have an overview of where to find certain types of sources.

WHERE DO I FIND IT?

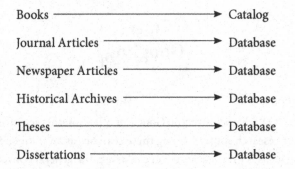

You'll notice most of the resources are located in your library's databases, which require some skill to access wisely, but don't worry. We will go over how to use both the databases and the library catalog.

FINDING "THEM" IN BOOKS AND ARTICLES

Scholarly sources typically exist in one of two forms:

1. Books

2. Articles in scholarly journals

What about newspapers and magazines, you ask? Most instructors consider newspaper and magazine articles to be *popular*, not scholarly, sources of information—in some cases, even highly regarded newspapers such as *The New York Times*. However, if you feel you have found an especially relevant, high-quality article that would work well in your paper, ask if you can use it. Every professor is different, and some may indeed allow it.

Check your sources for the following information:

	BOOKS	ARTICLES
DATE OF PUBLICATION AND CURRENCY	Is the material outdated or still relevant? (Some topics, but not all, require the most recent research.)	
AUTHOR CREDENTIALS	Look for a list of the author's credentials (university or college affiliation and expertise in the field). Fame or frequency of appearances on television does *not* constitute credentials.	
PUBLISHER/ EDITOR(S)	Look for a university press— these books are likely to be scholarly.	Look for university or college affiliation of the publication and/or its editor(s).
AUDIENCE	Look for books written for a specialized audience, not for mass consumption.	Look for articles written by and for experts—not for the general public.

	BOOKS	ARTICLES
PRESENTATION, ORGANIZATION, AND ADVERTISEMENTS	Examine the table of contents to evaluate the logic and organization of the book.	If you see ads present in the periodical, this publication is not likely scholarly.
RESEARCH INCLUDED	Look for a bibliography of sources cited and/or consulted—*all* scholarly books include this information. Examine this list to see if *these* sources are scholarly.	Look for a bibliography of sources cited and/or consulted—*all* scholarly articles include this information. Examine this list to see if *these* sources are scholarly.

AVOIDING "THE EXACTLY MYTH"

As you begin searching for your books and articles, remember to be creative in your search. Don't get bogged down in trying to find other scholars who discuss the exact topic and perspective that you are discussing.

In fact, this is one of the most common problems students encounter with finding research: They get stuck in The Exactly Myth.

> *The Exactly Myth is based on the following belief: All sources I quote in my essay must be written exactly on the topic and perspective that I research in my work.*

For example, Robin, who is writing about father/daughter relationships in *The Taming of the Shrew* and *10 Things I Hate About You*, believes the only sources she can cite must be about father/daughter relationships in *The Taming of the Shrew* and *10 Things I Hate About You*.

This is a false assumption. You do *not* have to cite only sources written on your exact topic or perspective. In fact, finding such sources that discuss *exactly* the perspective on which you write will prove a difficult, if not impossible, task!

The solution is to find sources that discuss *any* and all aspects of your project and *apply* them to your perspective. Aspects of your project include:

- The text itself (the book, short story, poem, painting, play, research study, film, television program, etc.)
- The author or creator of the work or works (poet, sculptor, painter, writer, director, producer, philosopher, scientist, etc.)
- The topic or theme (romantic love, beauty, nature, war, death, spirituality, father/daughter relationships, gender, race, etc.)
- The type, time period, and origin of your text (sixteenth-century British play, twentieth-century American film, twenty-first-century comedic American television sitcom, nineteenth-century French painting, twentieth-century American economic problems, etc.)

Research any or all of these aspects, and then tie the information to your ideas. In short, get creative with the sources you find and then simply explain how or why they relate to your thesis.

This is not an easy task, especially at first, so keep in mind your job is to answer these key questions:

- Why should I include this source?
- How does this scholar's idea or perspective relate to mine?

Remember, to successfully incorporate a source, you must justify why and how it connects to your ideas and perspective on the issue or text.

When searching for sources, remember to be creative—and think about *all* angles of your paper. The titles of the articles do *not* need to perfectly match your thesis or prompt to contain information you can cite and build on in your work.

The following screenshot shows a list of articles that Robin found in her initial search. We will discuss how to find articles in detail later in this chapter. For now, just read the titles and assess their potential usability.

| The first article looks promising; the summary indicates it will address both the film and the play. This one's an obvious match. | However, what about the next entry? Its title indicates it will focus on marriage, which may or may not help Robin. However, since she will address the outcomes of the characters (which, for the play's characters, includes marriage), this article might be worth perusing. |

Even if a source is not useful to you, it may lead you to another; the writer may cite a work you should explore, either in the text itself or in the References list, so check this page before discarding any sources.

FINDING "THEM" IN PRINT

Before you head to the library to find print-based sources, be sure you have all the necessary materials with you. If you created a binder, as suggested in chapter 5, bring this binder with you. If not, be sure you bring with you, at minimum, a copy of your assignment and your keyword list.

HOW TO FIND BOOKS

1. Log on to your library's website. Find the "Catalog." Once you find it, look for "advanced search" and select this option.

2. Read over your keyword sheet, and decide whether it is best to search by author, title, or subject.

3. Select the "Limit search to available items" function, choose whether you want to search by "Subject," "Author," or "Title," and then type in your keywords and hit the "enter" or "search" button.

4. A list of records will pop up for you. Don't worry if every title isn't exactly what you want; just read through them, and see how many might be usable. When you see one you'd like to read, look for a box entitled "mark" or "save" and select this option; this function allows you to save the title and citation information. If you can't find this function, ask for help; it's more than worth the effort to find because it saves you the trouble of writing all the citation information by hand.

5. Select the "e-mail citations" option; this handy function e-mails all the citation information to your inbox! This is a nice feature; it means you will always have the information where you can find and access it.

TIPS

- Note *where* each book is located. If your college or university has multiple libraries and/or multiple floors within the library, highlight the floor number or building name and location.

- Once you have the list of books you'd like to read through, make a plan of attack for retrieving them. For example, organize your titles by floor (get books on the second floor first and books on the sixth floor last or vice versa …). If you are not sure how to find books at the library, ask for assistance.

EXAMPLE

See the example below of Russell's search results for his topic, a minimum wage increase for tipped employees. He went to his college library's catalog and typed in "minimum wage" to see how many results this simple search yielded.

The catalog found fifty-two entries, which is a manageable number (much more manageable than two thousand ...)

The "Add to Folder" option allows you to save entries so you can view, print, or even e-mail the list to yourself. To save records, check the empty box below the number of each record you want to save. Then, click on the "Add to folder" or "Save to folder" icon.

The listings, called "records," contain each book's important information (the title, author, date of publication, and call letters). Click on the underlined title of the book to find a summary of the book's contents; this info will help you assess the book's usefulness to your project.

FINDING "THEM" IN DATABASES

Although books are usually located on the shelves of your library and you must physically go to the library to locate them, scholarly articles can be accessed through databases. This means you can go to the library and find them, or you can access them anywhere via an Internet connection.

"Wait," you may be thinking, "didn't we agree earlier that we shouldn't trust or use online sources?" Great question. The difference is that we are now finding sources online through the library, not through Google or other popular sources. This is not a minor detail; as we discussed earlier, sources found via the library must undergo rigorous academic scrutiny before publication; we have no idea what review process—if any—Internet sources undergo before they are posted.

HOW TO FIND JOURNAL ARTICLES

1. Log on to your college or university's library website. Locate the research database. It may be labeled "Journals," "Articles and Research," "Articles Search," or simply "Database."

2. Some libraries allow you to search all databases or to select specific databases. If you are forced to select a specific database and you have no idea which one to use, I suggest using one of these generic academic databases: Academic Search Premier, LexisNexis Academic, or EBSCOhost.

3. Read over your keyword list, and select the keywords you will enter into the search for articles. Remember, be specific, but not too specific, in your search. If the database offers the option of "full-text articles" only, select this option. If you do not get enough results, try deselecting it.

4. A list of records will pop up for you. Don't worry if every title isn't exactly what you need; just read through the titles and see how many might be usable. When you see one you'd like to read, look for a box labeled "mark" or "save"; this function allows you to save the title and citation information. If you can't find this function, ask for help; it's more than worth the effort to find, as it will save you from having to write out all your citation information.

5. Select the "e-mail citations" option; this handy function e-mails the information to your inbox.

If you have any trouble at all, don't be afraid to ask for help from librarians; they are hired to assist you! Keep them employed by asking for help. Most of them truly enjoy researching and can help you more than you might think.

EXAMPLE

Consider the following example of Robin's search for articles on father/daughter relationships in *The Taming of the Shrew* and *10 Things I Hate About You*.

Notice that the search box at the top of the page looks similar to the catalog's search box. Simply type in your topic, text, or both to see how many results you find.

Like a catalog search, the database search allows you to refine your results. Check any of these options to narrow your results. (The "full text" option will tell the database to list only articles you can access instantly.)

Many college and university libraries now offer a "search for articles" text box on their library home page, which allows you to simply type in your topic or text—and save the time of having to select a database. This function essentially means the library has selected the database for you, usually a general database that contains scholarly articles from multiple disciplines (in the case above, we see that this database is "Academic Search Complete").

If you must write on a highly specialized topic within a certain field, you may want to avoid the generic database on the library's home page and instead seek a discipline-specific database. For example, psychology students often use the PsycINFO® database, whereas literature students use the MLA International Bibliography database.

For general topics, however, usually one of the interdisciplinary databases, such as Academic Search Complete, JSTOR, and LexisNexis Academic, will work well.

If you have any questions regarding which database(s) to search, ask your instructor and/or a librarian.

MORE STRATEGIES FOR SEARCHING

If you are experiencing difficulty finding sources, don't give up. Finding strong sources requires creativity—and determination. Try any or all of the following strategies. Each strategy's effectiveness depends on your topic and texts, so if one does not work for you, skip to the next.

1. **TYPE IN THE TITLE OF ALL TEXTS TOGETHER.** For example, Robin, who is comparing father/daughter relationships in *The Taming of the Shrew* and *10 Things I Hate About You,* would simply type in "Taming of the Shrew and 10 Things I Hate About You."

   This is the most common strategy students use to find sources, which is fine, but it is certainly not the only strategy. Sometimes this type of search will yield entirely too many results, and other times it yields zero results. The latter usually confuses students, and thus they give up, thinking, "No one has ever written on this." They mistakenly conclude they cannot continue researching. If you find no articles or books that consider both of your texts, try the strategies below.

2. **TYPE IN THE TITLE OF EACH TEXT SEPARATELY.** For example, Robin would type in "Taming of the Shrew" and note the results. Then—on a separate search—she would type in "10 Things I Hate About You."

   A classic text like Shakespeare's *The Taming of the Shrew* will undoubtedly generate far too many results to handle. However, a search on a 1990s film adaptation geared to a teen audience (*10 Things I Hate About You*) will probably not, so Robin will get more manageable results by searching the film title.

3. **TYPE IN THE TITLE OF ALL TEXTS *AND* THE TOPIC.** For example, Robin would type in: "Taming of the Shrew *and* 10 Things I Hate About You *and* fathers *and* daughters."

This very narrow search will likely yield few, if any, results, but if another scholar has written on your precise texts and topics, you will definitely want to address her perspective in your essay!

4. **TYPE IN THE TITLE OF EACH TEXT *SEPARATELY* WITH YOUR TOPIC.** Try several variations of the word(s) associated with your topic. For example, Robin could type in "Taming of the Shrew and father" *or* "'Taming of the Shrew and fatherhood" *or* "Taming of the Shrew and father and daughter" *or* "10 Things I Hate About You and fatherhood" *or* "10 Things I Hate About You and father and daughter" *or* "10 Things I Hate About You and daughter."

5. **TYPE IN THE NAME OF ALL THE TEXTS' AUTHORS.** For example, Robin could type in "Shakespeare and Gil Junger." This search's effectiveness depends on the relative obscurity of the authors. Major writers (like Shakespeare) and their work (like *The Taming of the Shrew*) are often compared and contrasted with other texts (such as the film *10 Things I Hate About You*). If either of the authors are very prominent, you are much more likely to get better results. However, if you have two relatively obscure authors, you are unlikely to find an article or book discussing both.

6. **TYPE IN THE NAME OF EACH AUTHOR SEPARATELY.** For film texts, enter the name of the director and/or writers; for television programs, type in the name(s) of the producer(s) and/or writers.

   For example, Robin could type in "Shakespeare" in one search and "Gil Junger" in the next search.

   The first search will yield entirely too many results; scholars have penned thousands, even millions, of pages on Shakespeare, and trying to leaf through all of them will waste your time. However, the scholarship on a contemporary film director will be much less extensive and thus less daunting.

7. **TYPE IN THE NAME OF EACH AUTHOR TOGETHER WITH THE TOPIC.** For example, Robin could type in "Shakespeare and Gil Junger and fatherhood" or "Shakespeare and Gil Junger and daughters." This kind of search will likely be far too specific, but it might also yield interesting results.

8. **TYPE IN THE NAME OF EACH AUTHOR SEPARATELY, AND THEN ADD A TOPIC TO THE SEARCH.** For example, Robin could type in "fathers and Shakespeare" *or* "Gil Junger and fathers" *or* "Shakespeare and daughter" *or* "Gil Junger and daughters."

9. **TYPE IN ONLY YOUR TOPIC.** For example, Robin could type in "fathers and daughters." The first search will probably yield far too many results because it is too broad, but depending on the scope of your topic, sometimes this strategy can prove helpful.

10. **TYPE IN ONLY YOUR TOPIC AND THE TYPE(S) OF TEXTS AND/ OR TIME PERIODS YOU MUST EXAMINE.** For example, Robin could type in "film and fatherhood" *or* "fatherhood in teenage films" *or* "fatherhood in Renaissance theater" *or* "fatherhood in Renaissance literature" *or* "fathers and daughters in Renaissance" and so on.

TROUBLESHOOTING TIPS

Don't panic if you encounter problems during any part of the research process. Many students, even the most advanced ones, run into issues while researching. See the chart below for possible solutions.

PROBLEM	SOLUTION(S)
I can't find *anything!*	• Use more vague, general language in your search. • Try all three types of searches: author, subject, and title. • Remove quotation marks from your search if you used them. • Ask your professor or research librarian for help.
I found way too much information!	• Use more specific language in your search. • Place quotation marks around the phrase or subject as you search for it. • Choose the "advanced-search" option and use the "NOT" feature to eliminate irrelevant information.
Everything I found is "popular" and not scholarly.	Make sure you are not using Google, Bing, Yahoo, or others like them to find sources. Enlist the help of your librarian or professor. Bring whatever work you have found so far and a list of your methods, including your keyword list; this information will help them determine the root of the problem.
I found plenty of sources, but I'm having trouble understanding them.	See later in this chapter for a discussion on how to break down the books and articles and make them easier to understand.

PROBLEM	SOLUTION(S)
I can't decide which sources to use and which ones to discard.	This is actually a good "problem" to have. If you have so many sources you could use all of them, just select your favorite ones or the ones you can most easily quote. If you don't have a favorite and you could quote all of them, just choose. If you cannot make a decision, visit your instructor and ask her to help you choose.
I found plenty of books and articles on my text, but the scholars don't discuss exactly what I'm discussing.	Don't worry if your sources don't approach your text or topic *exactly* as you do. Sometimes you have to get creative to connect another person's ideas to yours. For a detailed discussion and examples of how to make these connections, see earlier in this chapter.

WHERE TO GET MORE RESEARCH HELP

If you're having trouble with your paper, don't suffer in silence! Take advantage of the many on-campus resources available to help you.

- **YOUR PROFESSOR:** When you have a problem, go to the source. Your instructor wrote the assignment and has likely already done extensive research on it himself, so go to his office hours or make an appointment to get help. Be sure to bring with you proof of your attempts to find sources; you don't want to make the professor think you want him to do your research for you.

- **RESEARCH LIBRARIANS:** The primary purpose of the research librarian is to help students do research. She will not do all of your work for you, but she will help get you started and answer questions while you're completing the job.

  You can go to the library in person or just visit your college or university library's web page. Most libraries have twenty-four-hour live chat services that provide answers from an expert immediately.

- **WRITING CENTER OR LEARNING LAB:** These excellent resources are *free* to students and typically offer direct, one-on-one counseling with graduate and upperclassmen who have plentiful research experience. This is a great way to meet other successful students and learn their tricks and strategies for getting great grades on research assignments and other types of assignments.

- **FELLOW CLASSMATES, FRIENDS, FAMILY MEMBERS, OR SIBLINGS:** *Use these resources sparingly;* many of your friends and classmates may *think* they know how to research effectively, but do you know for sure whether their advice is sound? You don't want to wait until you get your grade to find out. If you know an *A* student and you trust their opinion, then by all means enlist their help for your project, but always, always go to experts first. Your friend or sibling may or may not be an expert, so apply caution here.

UNDERSTANDING THE RESEARCH: SQ3R

If you're having trouble understanding the research you find, you are not alone. Many students have difficulty understanding other scholars' work, and this is indeed a serious issue, for if you do not understand their ideas, you cannot respond to and build on those ideas. Therefore, you can imagine how important it is to ensure that you do indeed understand the meaning of the work you cite in your essays.

When struggling with a difficult article or book, break down the text to make it less intimidating and more manageable. The "SQ3R" method, used extensively for decades, has helped millions of students break down challenging texts and understand them.

SQ3R:
Survey
Question
Read
Recite
Review

1. Before you read, Survey the book or article. Look specifically at the following elements of your research sources:

   - Book, article, or chapter title
   - Abstract or summary
   - Table of contents and major headings and subheadings
   - Introduction and conclusion paragraphs
   - Major charts, maps, diagrams, or graphs

   Write down the most important ideas or terms you notice. Once you feel you have an overview of the book or article, you can begin to read. Remember that you do *not* have to read an entire book to cite it in your paper; focus only on the most relevant chapter(s).

2. As you begin to read, ask Questions about the material. The questions you ask will depend on the type and level of material you read, but the following generic questions are always important to address:

- What is this author's major point?
- Who cares about this point? Why is it important?
- How does this information relate to my thesis?
- What major evidence does this author present?
- Do I agree with him? Why or why not?

Be sure to write down your answers to these questions.

3. After you finish Reading, you may want to recite and review what you've read to test whether you truly understand it or not. If not, you can always reread.

4. Recite what you've learned after you read a chapter or section. See it, say it, hear it, and write it. The more senses you engage with your reading, the more important your brain deems the material—and thus the better you will understand and remember it.

- **SEE IT:** Look again at the book or article and any important diagrams, images, or charts.
- **SAY IT:** Explain aloud what you read, either to someone else or just to yourself. (It may feel strange at first, but this is an immensely helpful way to ingrain the material!)
- **HEAR IT:** Listening to yourself explain will further impress the information into your brain.
- **WRITE IT:** Write down the most important points and your reaction to them.

5. Once you finish reading and reciting your sources, Review your notes, and then begin to pick out the most important elements. These crucial points will likely be the ones you insert into your paper.

If you complete these steps and still don't feel you truly understand your sources' ideas, gather your notes together and head to your professor's next open office hours. Ask her to help you with the research, and be prepared to show her what you've worked on so far.

If you're wondering whether deeply understanding the sources you cite really matters, you are, again, not alone. Many students mistakenly believe they can throw some quotes into their paper and still earn a good grade. As a grader of thousands of pages of research papers, I can assure you this is a strategy that will lead to a failing paper! You cannot examine, analyze, and respond to research if you don't yet understand it.

See also the T-notes and Research Templates sections on the following pages for further help with summarizing and understanding research.

T-NOTES

A T-note format can help you understand the research you encounter. There are several ways to use this format, two of which are listed below, but feel free to create and design your own methods for using the T-note.

T-NOTE "Q & A"

1. Get out a blank sheet of paper or open a blank Word document, and divide the page or screen into halves with a vertical line. On the left side of the page or screen, write or type "Questions" at the top; on the right side of the page or screen, write or type "Answers."

<table>
<tr><td>QUESTIONS</td><td>ANSWERS</td></tr>
</table>

2. Before you read, look at the title and quickly scan through the book or article and jot down any questions that come to mind about its ideas or how they relate to your ideas.

3. With your T-note nearby, read the article and write or type questions in the "Questions" column as they come to you. As you figure out the answers, write them inside the "Answers" column. When you finish reading, refer back to your T-note and see if you have any unanswered questions; if so, try to find the answers. If you cannot figure out the answers and you feel they are important enough to merit investigation, ask your instructor for help.

T-NOTE: "YOURS, MINE, AND OURS"

1. Get out a blank sheet of paper or open a blank Word document, and divide the page or screen into thirds. On the far left side of the page, write or type "Yours" at the top; in the middle column, write or type "Mine"; in the far right column, write or type "Ours."

YOURS	MINE	OURS

2. With your T-note nearby, read the article and write or type *the scholar's* arguments under the "Yours" column (it may help to write or type the scholar's name at the top of the column); write *your* opinion of their ideas or argument under the "Mine" column, and write any ideas you and the scholar share under "Ours."

The following is Robin's response to an article's discussion of the connections between Shakespeare's *The Taming of the Shrew* and the modern film adaptation *10 Things I Hate About You.*

YOURS (PITTMAN)	MINE	OURS
The film creates a backstory for Kat that "serves to underscore the quiet misogyny of the plot: girl traumatized by sex becomes frigid ice queen and requires a more satisfying sexual encounter to restore balanced personality" (p. 147)	Kat wasn't traumatized by having sex with Joey; in fact, it awakened her to her own extreme conformity to the whole teen culture or whatever Professor Brown called it (need to look this up!). Kat even says something like, "Everyone was doing it, so I did it," so she realized what a mistake it is to conform and she swore never to do that again. Her angry behavior has to do with her mom's leaving and her belief that her dad isn't proud of her.	
The film fails "to reconfigure gender roles" (p. 147)	I think the film does show how we've reconfigured gender. Kat isn't "tamed"; she's accepted for who she is, both by her dad and by Patrick. He doesn't do horrible things to her to try to "fix" her, and he doesn't make some bet with his male friends at the end to prove how obedient she is. He knows she's not perfect, but he likes her for who she is.	
Kat's dance at the keg party represents "the end of her critique of teens and its potent rules for behavior."	No. If she conformed to their rules for the rest of the movie, then, yeah, I'd agree, but the keg party scene shows Kat could conform to their rules and be like them if she wanted, but she chooses not to. She still criticizes the whole teen culture thing after that scene.	

Robin's T-note clearly reveals that she disagrees with the scholar's perspective of the film (she has no items in the "Ours" column). This information will help her set up the scholars' quotes within a *No* framework. (For more info on *No* frameworks, see chapter 7).

RESEARCH SUMMARY TEMPLATE

As you begin reading your sources, answer the following questions. The answers will create a research template that will summarize all the research you have read for your project. If you can't answer all the questions, don't worry; just do your best. Create one template for each source.

RESEARCH SUMMARY TEMPLATE

AUTHOR: _____

TITLE: _____

TYPE OF SOURCE (CIRCLE ONE):

Journal Article   Book   Newspaper Article

Other _____

MAJOR POINT(S) ARGUED:

MAJOR EVIDENCE PRESENTED:

MY OPINION OF THIS AUTHOR'S IDEAS AND EVIDENCE:

I MIGHT USE THIS ARTICLE IN MY ESSAY TO SHOW OR PROVE _____?

QUESTIONS I HAVE ABOUT THIS ARTICLE OR THE IDEAS IN IT:

If you thoroughly answered these questions about your research source, then you have successfully evaluated research.

Consider Russell's sample research template:

RESEARCH SUMMARY TEMPLATE

AUTHOR(S): Sylvia A. Allegretto and David Cooper

TITLE: Twenty-Three Years and Still Waiting for Change: Why It's Time to Give Tipped Workers the Regular Minimum Wage

TYPE OF SOURCE (CIRCLE ONE):

Journal Article   Book   Newspaper Article

Other _____   (Report)

MAJOR POINT(S) ARGUED:

They tie the rising income inequality to the tipped employee minimum wage. Over the past four decades, the "slow-down in improving American living standards has been driven by weak hourly wage growth" (p. 2).

Raising tipped workers' pay WON'T hurt businesses; these researchers looked at seven states where tipped workers receive the full regular minimum wage. The higher wage had "no discernable effect on leisure and hospitality employment growth . . . in fact, sector growth in these states has been stronger" (p. 4).

MAJOR EVIDENCE PRESENTED:

This article says that the full-service restaurant industry has grown over 85 percent since 1990. "More than one in ten U.S. workers is employed in the leisure and hospitality sector." So, they're super important because "making labor policies for these industries is central to defining typical American work life" (p. 2).

The tipped minimum wage has stayed at $2.13 since 1993. Then, it was 50 percent of regular minimum wage. Now, it's only 29.4 percent of the regular minimum wage. That's pathetic.

The poverty rate of tipped workers is twice as high as non-tipped ones, so almost half of them "rely on public benefits" (p. 3).

MY OPINION OF THIS AUTHOR'S IDEAS AND EVIDENCE:
Totally agree. It's unfair everybody else got a raise in their minimum hourly pay except for these people. Also, does "relying on public benefits" mean WE taxpayers are paying their benefits because the restaurant doesn't feel like it???

I MIGHT USE THIS ARTICLE IN MY ESSAY TO SHOW OR PROVE_____?
This article gives me a strong "who cares" because it shows why other people should care about how much money these restaurant workers make, like, how their pay affects the rest of us.

QUESTIONS I HAVE ABOUT THIS ARTICLE OR THE IDEAS IN IT:

None right now . . .

·➤· CHAPTER 7 ·◄·

Post-Research

YOUR IDEAS AND THEIR IDEAS

Now that you have read your research and understand it, how do you incorporate it into your essay?

▌ *Think of incorporation as **your response to their ideas**.*

The scholars stated their opinions and evidence on the issue, and now you will state yours. Remember, as a writer of collegiate-level work, you are entering the academic conversation (The Great Debate). Now that you've read the scholars' "cases" on the issue(s) you researched, you must address two key questions: Are you convinced by their argument and evidence? Why or why not? You will likely have one of three answers: Yes, No, or Maybe.

It is extremely important to address *why* you agree, disagree, or remain uncertain. If you agree, why? If you disagree, why? If you remain uncertain, why?

You'll find on the following pages a discussion of each of these responses and how to verbalize them. However, the following rules of thumb will provide you with an overall guide for successfully incorporating the work of others into your essays.

RULES OF THUMB:
INCORPORATING THE WORK OF
OTHERS INTO YOUR ESSAY

1. IMMEDIATELY STATE YOUR OPINION OF THE SCHOLAR'S THEORY, IDEA, OR WORK. Do you agree (yes), disagree (no), or remain uncertain (maybe) about their major contention? Why?

2. DO NOT BE VAGUE ABOUT YOUR OPINION. Many students make the mistake of keeping the reader guessing or "saving" their evaluation of the research for "later."

Academics don't view vagueness as an invitation to keep reading; they see it as weak, inadequate writing. Academics expect authors to state their perspective immediately and spend the bulk of the essay defending and explaining that position.

3. ALWAYS EXPLAIN AND DEFEND YOUR POSITION, REGARDLESS OF YOUR STANCE. Whether you take a position of yes, no, or maybe, you must cite evidence to support and explain your stand.

YES: EXPRESSING AGREEMENT

Many students believe that agreeing with the scholars they cite will prove to be the easiest move, so this is indeed the position they take. They feel if they agree, they can simply state their agreement with the position or theory and move on. However, a simple statement of agreement does not constitute *evaluation*. Stating an opinion is only the first step in evaluation; once you determine your position on the issue, you must construct your defense of this opinion.

> *Examine the argument and its evidence closely; then, point out* **which specific elements** *prove its validity, establish its legitimacy, or point to its overall merit.*

Remember, you don't necessarily have to agree 100 percent with every idea or piece of evidence the scholar presents. Consider whether, *overall*, you find the scholar's major point or argument valid, interesting, or insightful.

A *Yes* response to an author's work may come in several forms:

- Complete, 100 percent agreement with the entirety of his work
- Overall agreement with most of the work
- Partial agreement with several major points within the work

These responses include the obvious *Yes* and also:

- Yes, but ...
- Yes, except for ...
- Yes, if ...
- Yes, assuming ...
- Yes, unless ...

> **Don't forget your "Because ...":** *Always state why you agree with the argument.*

Some of the most prominent reasons for agreement with a scholar's argument or perspective include the following. Cite these reasons, or add your own:

- Convincing argument
- Interesting, innovative argument
- Strong, substantial evidence to support the argument
- Accurately documented results and research
- Clearly organized
- Well-written work that illustrates the author's expertise and depth of knowledge on the subject
- Excellent, impassioned use of language and rhetoric

Below you will find examples of ways to express your agreement with other scholars' work and why you support their ideas.

YES: WHY	SUGGESTED ACADEMIC TRANSLATION(S)
"This scholar is brilliant!" **ASK YOURSELF:** *What* specific ideas or theories do you see as brilliant? Can you be more specific than "brilliant"? Do you mean the scholar has discovered new, irrefutable evidence? Perhaps her argument is constructed so well that it practically argues itself? Point to *specific element(s)* of the argument or theory you find so valuable or convincing and explain *why*.	• Jones discusses _____ in innovative, insightful ways that few other scholars have. Instead of _____, she _____. • Jones's argument proves overwhelmingly convincing because _____. • The evidence Smith presents undoubtedly proves her point because _____. • Few readers will likely argue with Smith's theory that _____ because she _____.

YES: WHY	SUGGESTED ACADEMIC TRANSLATION(S)
"I agree with Wilson, but I also disagree with him." **ASK YOURSELF:** With which *specific points* do you agree, and with which do you disagree? *Why?*	• Wilson first argues_____, and indeed he is correct because _____. However, when he later states, _____, he misses the mark because _____. • Yes, Wilson's finding of _____ is accurate; however, his presentation of _____ is not because _____. • Though Wilson makes an excellent point about _____, his evidence on _____ lacks credibility because _____. • Wilson's argument of _____ stands up to scrutiny. He rightly points out _____, but then later on page _____, he states, "_____," which illustrates that he fails to consider _____.

BEYOND THE CLASSROOM

New employees often think simply agreeing with the boss's opinion is the way to ensure a promotion or raise. But this is not always the case. When you do agree with your boss, state *why* you agree and cite evidence that illustrates the validity of the perspective. Don't be afraid to apply the *No* and *Maybe* strategies to your workplace conversations, too. Employees who illustrate their intelligence and capabilities are much more likely to garner raises and promotions than those who merely state their agreement with their supervisors' ideas but never offer any of their own.

NO: EXPRESSING DISAGREEMENT

Many students worry about taking a position of disagreement with scholars because they think that if they disagree, their instructor may see this disagreement as haughtiness on the part of the student and punish them in the form of a low score. Remember, you're not criticizing or evaluating the value of the scholar; you are evaluating the strength, merit, and significance of the scholar's work. You have every right—and responsibility—to state your opinion, including one of disagreement, if that is your honest perspective on the work.

This point is a good one to keep in mind as a writer, too; when your professors criticize your ideas, they are evaluating *your work*, not *you*. Your value as a student, as a person, is not in question. However, the value of your work is, and this point is true for the scholars whose work you examine.

Remember, you do not have to disagree 100 percent with every idea or piece of evidence the scholar presents. Consider whether, *overall*, you find the scholar's major point or argument invalid, inaccurate, or illogical.

A *No* response to an author's work may come in several forms:

- Complete 100 percent disagreement with the entirety of the work
- Overall disagreement with most of the work
- Disagreement with several major points within the work

> **Don't forget your "Because ...":** *Always state why you disagree with the argument.*

These responses include the obvious *No* and also:

- No, but ...
- No, except for ...
- No, unless ...
- No, assuming ...
- No, if ...

Some of the most prominent reasons for disagreement with a scholar's argument or perspective include the following. Cite these reasons, or add your own:

- Failure to present a convincing argument
- Boring, expected, trite, or hackneyed argument
- Weak, insubstantial evidence to support the argument
- Lack of or inaccurate documentation of the results
- Lack of or inaccurate citation of sources
- Lack of a central thesis and working structure
- Poorly written work that fails to illustrate the author's expertise and depth of knowledge on the subject
- Unclear, confusing language and jargon employed throughout the work

Below you will find examples of ways to express your disagreement with other scholars' work and why you oppose their ideas.

NO: WHY	SUGGESTED ACADEMIC TRANSLATION(S)
"No way. This is just stupid." **ASK YOURSELF:** *What* is stupid, exactly? Is the entire argument stupid or just one particular idea or argument? Figure out specifically *which elements* of the argument you feel are unintelligent and explain *why.* Perhaps you feel the evidence lacks credibility?	• The argument Smith presents fails logically because _____. • Smith's argument remains unconvincing because _____. • The evidence Smith presents lacks credibility because _____.

NO: WHY	SUGGESTED ACADEMIC TRANSLATION(S)
"Is this guy crazy? He's contradicting himself." **ASK YOURSELF:** What is his overall argument and what *specific sentences* contradict his overall argument? Specify when/how the author contradicts himself. Then, address *why* you feel this contradiction makes his overall argument unconvincing, and perhaps confusing, for readers.	• Brown first argues _____; however, he then argues _____. This contradiction shows his thinking on _____ is wrought with errors because _____. • Brown's argument cannot be trusted; he vacillates on the issue of _____. He first states, "_____," but then later, on page _____, he states, "_____."
"Really? He wrote a research paper about this? My ten-year-old sister knows that." **ASK YOURSELF:** Outline specifically what parts of the author's argument you find are conventional wisdom or common knowledge. Then, point out what the writer *should* have addressed within the topic.	• Martin attempts to argue _____, but in fact _____ has been widely discussed by _____, _____, and _____. What Martin neglected to examine is _____. • Martin writes about _____ as though he presents to readers startling information, but, in fact, readers even vaguely familiar with _____ already understand _____. What Martin fails to discuss is the more important issue of _____.

MAYBE: EXPRESSING UNCERTAINTY

Many students either forget about or purposefully avoid the *Maybe* response. Many professors will allow or even encourage students to take a *Maybe* position on an issue, as long as the student makes clear why they find too much uncertainty surrounding a topic or issue to take a definitive stance.

However, taking a *Maybe* stance does not exempt you from presenting and evaluating evidence. In fact, the *Maybe* paper will likely argue two positions: the *Yes* and the *No*. If the essay's position is *Maybe*, the writer will need to show why both *Yes* and *No* may be valid responses but in different areas or ways.

Please note the following cautions concerning *Maybe*:

1. Not all professors allow the *Maybe* paper; be sure to ask before taking the time to write it.
2. Taking a *Maybe* stance can be a bit boring for a reader. After all, you are not arguing *Yes* or *No* definitively; you are essentially shrugging your shoulders and saying the answer is not yet evident. This perspective is perfectly fine, and indeed it is possible to make it interesting, but just keep in mind that it can often be more of a challenge, especially for beginning writers, to make the *Maybe* response as interesting as a direct *Yes* or *No*.

If after reading these cautions you are not deterred from your *Maybe* stance, then by all means, proceed. *Maybe* is an important answer, especially within the philosophy and medical fields.

A *Maybe* response to an author's work may come in several forms:

- Agreement with one aspect of her argument or analysis but disagreement with her overall conclusions or thesis
- Agreement with most of the argument itself but concern over the validity or accuracy of the evidence presented

> **Don't forget your "Because ...":** *Always state the reasons for your uncertainty with the scholar's argument and/or evidence.*

Some of the most prominent reasons for uncertainty regarding a scholar's argument or perspective include the following. Cite these reasons, or add your own:

- Convincing argument presented but the writer needs to cite more evidence to support it
- Interesting argument presented but the validity and credibility of the evidence cited remains in question
- Inadequate documentation of results or evidence
- Central thesis with interesting points but much of the work is confusing and difficult to understand or follow

Below you will find some of students' most common *Maybe* reactions to the research they encounter and suggestions about how to formalize and specify your opinion for your essay.

MAYBE: WHY	SUGGESTED ACADEMIC TRANSLATION(S)
"Well, yeah, I'd agree with that if ..." **ASK YOURSELF:** Specifically *which elements* of the argument do you feel lack credibility or validity? What evidence or point could the author interject that *would* convince you?	• Cohen's point may be valid; however, _____. • Although Cohen rightly points out _____, his overall argument of _____ fails to convince because _____. • Cohen's argument about _____, though interesting, remains unconvincing overall because he fails to address _____.

MAYBE: WHY	SUGGESTED ACADEMIC TRANSLATION(S)
"This article started out interesting, but then it got weird and confusing." **ASK YOURSELF:** What specific points within the book or article were "weird," and what do you mean by "weird"? Do you mean the point presented seems off-topic in relation to the author's overall discussion?	• The first few pages of Smith's article prove interesting and insightful in that she illustrates _____. However, as the article progresses, her discussion on _____ seems to veer off topic because she _____. • Although Smith had a valid point about _____, she quickly lost credibility on page _____ as she began to discuss _____.
"I disagree with almost everything she wrote, but at the end she finally says something right!" **ASK YOURSELF:** What specific point did the writer present that proved convincing to you? Why do you disagree with her other points or evidence?	• It's difficult to take a clear stand on Smith's work. Her argument on _____ proves invalid because _____. However, near the end of the article, she points out _____, and her evidence of _____ is indeed convincing.

SELECTING RELEVANT QUOTES

Once students find and formulate a response to scholarly sources, they often have trouble selecting quotes from within those sources. With such long articles or entire books looming before them, they wonder how they will choose particular sentences to insert into their paper.

Only quote what you can explain and defend.

In other words, always have a reason for why you chose the particular quote(s) you cite.

DEFENDING AND SELECTING YOUR QUOTES

Tie all quotes directly and clearly to your claim, and always explain each quote's significance. Never assume your reader understands the quote's significance or that its relevance "speaks for itself." Usually it does not.

Remember, the key to selecting quotes is *relevance*. Always have a justification for your inclusion of any quote(s). Ask and answer the following questions:

1. How is this quote relevant to your discussion?
2. Why does it go in the precise position in which you placed it in your paper?

Your answers to these questions will form the "E" (Explanation) section of your essay. It may help to review the sections on "I" and "E" in chapter 3.

PARAPHRASING VS. QUOTING

Paraphrasing sources allows more of your thinking to come through. Remember, your readers are seeking *your* words, not someone else's. Don't bury your ideas beneath a heap of quotations. Instead, use quotations to support and prove your point.

You should quote:

- When a character or writer's specific language or phrasing matter

- When language is particularly eloquent, impassioned, or significant

In other words, *quote* when the specific wording or phrasing is significant. You should paraphrase:

- When referring to an overall point or assertion of a text
- When referring to a specific event in the text

In other words, *paraphrase* when the specific wording or phrasing is not necessarily significant but the overall summary or point is.

Study Russell's example below, which demonstrates the debate of whether to paraphrase or quote.

> **William Buckley points out "the reasons we don't complain" (201).**

In this example, Russell unnecessarily included a direct quote. He may simply refer to the text's major point or claim, which in this case seems to be reasons people do not complain. However, what are these reasons? Do the particular reasons matter, or is Russell merely pointing out that Buckley raises the issue? He must explain the significance of this point and why Buckley raises it in his paper.

See Russell's rewrite below.

> **William Buckley points to the various reasons we do not complain—such as fear of others' reactions and sheer laziness—to make a larger point about overall American complacency and its connection to wide-scale injustice within our society.**

Russell decided to paraphrase rather than use a direct quote, which seems appropriate given that he largely summarizes Buckley's overall argument. He clearly feels the larger point of Buckley's essay was more important than any single phrasing he used. Russell has also done a nice job of pointing out Buckley's "So what?" which is that Americans' failure to complain has led to injustices in our society. However, Russell now must tie Buckley's point to his own.

> William Buckley points to the various reasons we do not complain—such as fear of others' reactions or sheer laziness—to make a larger point about overall American complacency and its connection to wide-scale injustice within our society. Indeed, Buckley has a point worth noting in terms of considering the low wages of tipped employees and the failure of restaurant workers to complain about their unfair, unethical treatment by powerful restaurant chains and their lobbyists.

There is not necessarily a right or wrong answer when determining whether to use direct quotes or paraphrases. Another student may have elected to quote Buckley directly, and this decision would be fine, as long as they explained the quote's significance to their own ideas.

INCORPORATE THEIR IDEAS
INTO YOURS: YES

The example below is taken from a student's paragraph in which she agrees with the scholar's work she cites. See the notes in the margin for commentary on the student's work.

The student names the author she will cite and offers a direct, relevant quote from the work.

The student then uses the word indeed and one of the suggested yes templates ("... few readers would likely disagree with ...") to indicate her agreement with the scholar.

She then cites her own evidence and explains why she agrees with the scholar.

Sharon Hamilton argues in her book *Shakespeare's Daughters* that Baptista is a lot like King Lear; to both fathers, image is more important than the relationship with his daughters. She writes, "Above all, each man values reputation and status and eschews any word or act that reflects badly on his public image, and the shallowness of their outlook is revealed by the presence of a sister who is the favored daughter's temperamental opposite" (93). Indeed, few readers would likely argue with Hamilton that Baptista is selfish and values his reputation more than he values his daughters because the man he allows to marry his oldest daughter, Petruchio, is a man he meets only for a few minutes—a man he does not know at all, yet he is happy to sell off Kate to this guy just because he thinks Petruchio has money. When meeting Baptista, Petruchio quickly tells Baptista he is Antonio's son, "A man well-known throughout all Italy" (II.ii.69.), and Baptista responds favorably to this name-dropping, saying he knows *of* Antonio, which in this time period basically meant Baptista knew of Antonio's wealth .... .

INCORPORATE THEIR IDEAS INTO YOURS: NO

This example is taken from a student's paragraph in which she disagrees with the scholar whose work she cites.

Mr. Unhae Langis claims that "virtue is the key guiding force in Petruchio's wooing and socializing of Kate" (48). However, this argument fails logically because Petruchio's actions defy the very meaning of the word *virtue*. Petruchio humiliates, brainwashes, and starves Kate; he even admits he treats her like an animal, like a falcon he plans to "tame." Clearly, Petruchio's actions are disturbing and cruel, and to a modern audience even criminal, but certainly not virtuous. Langis tries to justify his view by bringing up Aristotle and saying that Petruchio's methods are directed toward "salutary and excellent ends" and "the taming works both ways" (48). However, Langis's argument remains unconvincing because the very concept of "taming" someone is necessarily lacking in virtue. Plus, Langis gives no evidence to show how Kate supposedly tames Petruchio.

Notice the student names the author she will cite and offers a direct, relevant quote from the work.

The student then uses the word however followed by a suggested no template ("... this argument fails logically because ...") to signal her disagreement with the scholar's first point. She then goes on to debunk yet another point posited by the scholar to support her own claim that Kate's end is horrific.

She then cites her own evidence to explain why she disagrees with the scholar.

INCORPORATE THEIR IDEAS
INTO YOURS: MAYBE

Notice the student names the author he will cite and offers a direct, relevant quote.

The student then uses the word although *and one of the suggested* maybe *templates ("... his point fails to consider ... .") to indicate his uncertainty about the scholar's perspective.*

He then cites his own ideas to explain why he remains uncertain about the scholar's argument.

Economist Walter John Wessels is against raising the minimum wage for tipped employees because he warns us that raising it will actually lead to higher unemployment for these workers. According to him, "Consumers will substitute away from tipped-labor-intensive meals towards less expensive meals" and "eat out less, buying fewer restaurant meals of all types" (3). Wessels presents an interesting case, and although his point about higher meal prices may be valid, it fails to consider choice. Isn't raising prices simply a decision on the part of the restaurant owner and whether or not to eat out the choice of the diner? First, restaurants don't have to raise their prices so much that people no longer want to eat out; owners can choose to make just a little less money to help accommodate the new wage. Second, if restaurant customers are willing to pay just a little more to support the employees, then everyone can benefit. The extra income the employees earn will be circulated into the economy, which helps everyone. If people will make these choices to support these employees, I think Wessels's dire predictions might not come true.

ESSENTIAL WRITING SKILLS FOR COLLEGE & BEYOND

CITING THEIR IDEAS

Once you have found, evaluated, and incorporated your sources, you must cite them.

Academic essays require writers to cite sources in two ways:

- In-text or parenthetical citations
  &
- Works Cited or Bibliography page

You will find further discussion of how to cite parenthetically and on the Works Cited page in the following pages. However, before you start the citation process, be sure you know **which citation form or style your instructor requires**. Your prompt sheet should include directions that dictate which style to use. If not, ask your instructor.

Below you will find the three most common types of citation forms and the disciplines that typically use them:

- **MLA (MODERN LANGUAGE ASSOCIATION)**
  - The Humanities
  - Language and Literature
  - Gender and Cultural Studies
  - Art History
  - Film and Television Studies (may use Chicago style, too, so ask)
  - Advertising
  - Philosophy (may use Chicago style, too, so ask)

- **APA (AMERICAN PSYCHOLOGICAL ASSOCIATION):** Social and Behavioral Sciences
  - Psychology and Sociology
  - Education
  - Linguistics
  - Business and Economics
  - Nursing

- **CHICAGO STYLE (*THE CHICAGO MANUAL OF STYLE*)**
  - History (may also use MLA or APA, so ask)
  - Information Science
  - Philosophy
  - Communications and Journalism
  - Film and Television Studies (may also use MLA or APA, so ask)

CREATING IN-TEXT OR PARENTHETICAL CITATIONS

The parenthetical or in-text citation is exactly what it sounds like: It is a citation writers insert into the actual text of their essay (inside parentheses).

Each reference or source you cite in your essay corresponds to an entry on your Works Cited or References or Bibliography page.

To get started, follow the steps below to ensure you properly cite sources within the text of your essay.

STEP 1: CITE THE SOURCE AS YOU USE IT—IN THE BODY OF THE ESSAY.

Usually, this citation involves simply writing the author's last name and the page number *inside* the parentheses. However, some sources (especially Web sources) are more difficult to cite, so be sure to consult the proper style manual or website (MLA, APA, or Chicago, etc.) for examples on how to cite properly.

STEP 2: BE SURE ALL SOURCES CITED IN YOUR ESSAY GAIN A LISTING ON YOUR WORKS CITED OR BIBLIOGRAPHY OR REFERENCES PAGE.

After you cite your sources in the text, you will create a page at the end of your document that lists *all* of the sources you cite in the essay's body. (We'll go over how to create this document on the following pages.)

TO CITE OR NOT TO CITE . . .

This is indeed the question for many students; they wonder whether they should cite *every* source they found or not. Just remember that *anytime you reference, mention, or in any way use or consult the work of another scholar, you must cite their work.*

Do not fear over-citing!

If you are uncertain about whether to cite, then go ahead and cite the source, just to be safe. If you cite it, but you did not need to do so, the worst punishment you incur will be the loss of a few points. However, if you do NOT cite when you should have, you may face charges of plagiarism—a serious academic offense. (For more info on plagiarism, see page 253.) To be safe, follow the rule below:

> **When in doubt, cite.** *It's better to cite unnecessarily than to omit the citation when you needed it.*

If you found a source while researching but did not at all use it, then you do not need to cite it. However, if your ideas *in any way* are based on that scholar's work, then you need to cite them.

See the following pages and the MLA, APA, and Chicago style handbooks for further examples . . .

EXAMPLES

Study the following brief examples to gain an overview of parenthetical citations in the two most common styles: MLA and APA. For further examples, see the appropriate style manual (MLA, APA, or Chicago).

Also, note that the MLA, APA, and Chicago style manuals are updated periodically, so *always* check the most recent edition to ensure your citations are 100 percent up to date.

EXAMPLE 1: MLA

INCORRECT: In her book *Shakespeare's Daughters*, Sharon Hamilton claims, "Nowhere is Shakespeare more astute than in his portrayal of fathers and daughters and the factors that foster or undermine that bond" (Hamilton p. 2).

Since the student already mentioned the author's name, there's no need to include it inside the parenthetical citation. Also, remove the "p." before the page number. ONLY the actual page number or numbers are required for MLA citations.

CORRECT: In her book *Shakespeare's Daughters*, Sharon Hamilton claims, "Nowhere is Shakespeare more astute than in his portrayal of fathers and daughters and the factors that foster or undermine that bond" (2).

ALSO CORRECT: Indeed, "Nowhere is Shakespeare more astute than in his portrayal of fathers and daughters and the factors that foster or undermine that bond" (Hamilton 2).

Notice in the second correct example above that we added the author's name to the parenthetical citation. Why? Since we did not mention the author in our quote, we'll need to cite their last name along with the page number. Whether you cite the author in your actual text or the citation is up to you. Try both methods and see which achieves greater flow or stronger effect. (Ask a peer, or test it by reading each aloud.)

EXAMPLE 2: APA

INCORRECT: Economist David Cooper's research shows that raising the minimum wage would "increase U.S. GDP by about $22 billion, thus resulting in the creation of roughly 85,000 net new jobs" (Cooper, p. 3).

The student already listed the author's name in the sentence, so there's no need to include the name *again* inside the parentheses. Also, APA rules require us to cite *the date* of the publication.

CORRECT: Economist David Cooper's (2013) research shows that raising the minimum wage would "increase U.S. GDP by about $22 billion, thus resulting in the creation of roughly 85,000 net new jobs" (p. 3).

ALSO CORRECT: Raising the minimum wage would "increase U.S. GDP by about $22 billion, thus resulting in the creation of roughly 85,000 new jobs" (Cooper, 2013, p. 3).

Notice in the second correct example, we added the author's name to the citation rather than mentioning it in our text. Students often ask which way is better, and although it depends on context, if you're citing a well-known, highly respected expert in the field, keep their name in your text so readers don't miss it. This strategy demonstrates your knowledge of top thinkers in the field—and it highlights that you have decidedly credible support for your case.

USING AUTOMATIC CITATION SOFTWARE OR APPS

In recent years, a plethora of automatic citation generators have flooded the market, purporting to help college students cite their sources properly. Yet, you may be wondering: Are they trustworthy . . . and . . . should you use them?

The answer is: It depends.

It depends on your instructor and/or class, the auto generator you're using, and whether you want/need to learn to cite sources for yourself.

If your instructor is quite strict about citation formats and expects 100 percent accuracy, it's probably fine to use these auto generators as a jumping-off point, but don't rely on them exclusively. Check and double-check your citations before turning in the final essay. If, on the other hand, your instructor simply wants you to gain some practice with the idea of finding and citing sources, then you might be fine using the auto generators. Any errors that occur as a result will likely be forgiven.

Also consider which auto generator to use and your level of certainty in its accuracy. Not all generators are created equally, and probably none offer 100 percent accuracy.

So, if you do use the auto generator:

1. **Use with caution.**
ALWAYS double check the citations with the most updated MLA, APA, or Chicago handbook before turning in the final draft.

2. **Don't rely exclusively on the auto citation generators.**
They can be a huge help with citing, especially to get you started, but don't rely entirely upon them. Ask your instructor, TA, and/or research librarian for help, too. They can help spot any errors the auto generators might miss . . .

Some students skip the auto generators completely because they simply prefer to create the citations themselves, especially for classes in their major. Yet, if you and your instructor are okay with using auto citation generators, do your research and discover which offer the highest level of accuracy.

To help in this vein, check out these possible auto generators:

- EasyBib
- Style Wizard
- Citation Machine
- Opendemia
- Cite This For Me
- BibMe
- Citefast
- Zotero

The above sites have proven relatively accurate in the past, but you might also inquire with your instructor and/or TA for their preferred list as well.

Remember to use caution with these generators.

The formatting can be particularly troublesome, as it often becomes corrupted between the generator's cite and the Word or Google document into which you paste the text. Line spacing and indenting often do not translate perfectly, so double-check the citations before you turn in the final draft of the essay!

CREATING A WORKS CITED OR REFERENCES PAGE

The parenthetical references you cite within the body of your text refer your reader to the final page of your document: In other words, it gives the reader a list of all sources referenced within the essay. We call this list a Works Cited or References page. All serious scholars must include such a page to prove they used the work of experts to support and create their own. You, too, must include such a page if you cite, consult, or in any way use or reference the work of others.

Remember the Golden Rule for creating the Works Cited page: Ensure your list adheres to the style of the discipline for which you are writing (MLA style for English, APA style for psychology, Chicago style for communication, etc).

> *Most libraries offer citation functions that will format your sources into the appropriate citation style, so it is probably not necessary for you to spend hours poring over a style manual.*

To use the citation feature:

1. Click on the book or article's title from the listing within the database.
2. Scan the page for the citation function; look for the word *cite* or *citation*; usually you'll find it on the right-hand side of the screen.
3. Click on this icon, and select your citation style (MLA, APA, or Chicago). Copy and paste the citation, and insert it into your essay's Works Cited or Reference page.

Even with these handy citation functions, you will need to have general knowledge of the style's rules so you can check the work of the computer's citation functions. Few citation functions actually cite sources 100 percent accurately, so always check their work before you submit your essay.

CITATION FORMULAS FOR WORKS CITED OR REFERENCES PAGES

Whether you title your final page "Works Cited," "References," or "Bibliography" will depend upon the discipline for which you write. Academics typically use the term "Works Cited" when citing sources with MLA format, "References" when citing sources using APA format, and "Bibliography" or "References" when citing with Chicago style.

When in doubt, ask your instructor or consult your MLA, APA, or Chicago style manual for the most updated information and examples. See below for formulas for the most frequently used formats.

MLA FORMULAS

A BOOK (WITH ONLY ONE AUTHOR)*

Author's Last Name, First Name. *Title of Book*. Publisher, Year of

Publication.

EXAMPLE:

Gill, Charlene. *College Success for Adults: Insider Tips for Effective*

Learning. Routledge, 2020.

Note: Add the city of publication *ONLY* if the book was published before 1900, if the publisher has offices in multiple countries, or if the publisher is unknown in North America. Otherwise, no need to include the city of publication.

A BOOK (WITH TWO AUTHORS)

> First Author's Last Name, First Name, and Second Author's First
>
> Name Last Name. *Title of Book*. Publisher, Year of Publica-
>
> tion. Location.

EXAMPLE:

> King, Stephen, and Peter Straub. *The Talisman*. Viking, 1984.

AN ARTICLE IN A SCHOLARLY JOURNAL

> Author's Last Name, First Name. "Main Title of Article: Subtitle
>
> of Article." *Title of Journal*, volume, number or issue, year,
>
> pages.

If you accessed the article via a database, add the location, meaning the title of the database (such as JSTOR, etc.) and the URL/DOI *after* the page numbers.

A **URL** (Uniform Resource Locator) is essentially just the **location** or **web address** that identifies **where you found the source online.** It could be, for example, http://www.exampleURL.com. Citing this address or location is critical so your readers can easily find and check your source(s).

A **DOI** (Digital Object Identifier) is a unique combination of numbers, letters, and symbols that identifies an article or document online. The DOI basically provides the article with a permanent web address (URL) so your readers can easily access and verify its contents. You might think of the DOI as akin to the document's social security number because it identifies that document—and *only* that one—so the article doesn't get lost in cyberspace.

EXAMPLE DOI:

10.1111/josi.12122

TO FIND THE DOI:

- Check the article itself. Usually, it's printed on the first page below the title or in the header or footer.
- If the DOI isn't listed in the article, look it up on CrossRef.org (use the "Search Metadata" option) and check for an assigned DOI.
- Not all articles have DOIs, so if there truly is no DOI available, just use the URL.

EXAMPLE:

Benton, Mark. "Public Justifications for the U.S. Minimum Wage."

Industrial Relations Journal, vol. 52, no. 4, 2021, pp. 331–347.

https://onlinelibrary.wiley.com/doi/abs/10.1111/irj.12338.

A BOOK CHAPTER

Author's Last Name, First Name. "Title of Chapter." *Title of Book*

or Collection, edited by Editor's First Name Last Name(s),

Publisher, year, page ranges of chapter.

EXAMPLE:

Green, David."Supporting the Academic Success of Hispanic

Students." *College Libraries and Student Culture: What We*

Now Know, edited by Andrew D. Asher and Lynda M. Duke,

American Library Association, 2011, pp. 87–108.

APA FORMULAS

A BOOK (WITH ONLY ONE AUTHOR)

Author Last Name, First Initial. Middle Initial. (Year of publica-

tion). *Book title*. Publisher. DOI (if available)

EXAMPLE:

Lewis, R. G. (2020). *Color psychology: Profit from the psychol-*

ogy of color: Discover the meaning and effects of color.

Nielsen.

ARTICLE IN A PRINT JOURNAL

Author Last Name, First Initial. Middle Initial., & Second Author's

Last Name, First Initial. Middle Initial. (Year of publication).

Title of article. *Title of Journal, volume number*(issue num-

ber), page numbers. DOI

EXAMPLE:

Mellers, B.A. (2001). Choice and the relative pleasure of conse-

quences. *Psychological Bulletin, 126*(1), 919–924.

ARTICLE IN AN ELECTRONIC JOURNAL

> Author Last Name, First Initial. Middle Initial., & Second Author's
>
> Last Name, First Initial. Middle Initial. (Year of publication).
>
> Title of article. *Title of Journal, volume number*(issue num-
>
> ber), page numbers. DOI or URL

EXAMPLE:

> Bernardon, S., Babb, K. A., Hakim-Larson, J. & Gragg, M. (2011).
>
> Loneliness, attachment, and the perception and use of social
>
> support in university students. *Canadian Journal of Behav-*
>
> *ioural Science, 43*(1), 40–51. https://doi.org/10.1037/a0021199

What if your article does *not* have a DOI?

1. If you retrieved it from a subscription-based research database (such as EBSCO, JSTOR, or Psychinfo, etc.), provide the author, date, title, and periodical information *only*. Your reference will thus end with the page range.

   Or

2). If you retrieved your article from the web (*not* from a database), then just use the URL instead of a DOI.

   For further info and examples, see the APA handbook, p. 299.

FOR APA CITATIONS, REMEMBER:

1. The titles of articles in APA style **no longer require quotation marks**.

2. **Watch your capitalization** of words within titles in APA.
   Only capitalize
   a) The first word of the title
   b) Proper nouns in the title
   c) The first word of the subtitle
3. DOIs (Digital Object Identifiers) may not always be available. When they're not, **just use a URL.**

MORE EXAMPLES

Let's take a look now at a few examples of Works Cited pages with multiple entries so you can see what the final product might look like . . .

EXAMPLE 1: INCORRECT MLA WORKS CITED PAGE

Works Cited

> Hamilton, Sharon. Shakespeare's Daughters. Jefferson, N. C.: Mc-Farland, 2003. Print.

> Gay, Penny. As She Likes It: Shakespeare's Unruly Women. London: Routledge, 2002. Print.

What's wrong with the entries on this Works Cited page? The writer must

1. *Double space—within each listing AND* between items in the list.
2. *Alphabetize* the list by author's last names; if the entry has no listed author, simply alphabetize by the first letter of the entry.
3. *Indent second lines* of citations by .5 inches. (Hit the "tab" key.)
4. *Remove the reference to the source as "print."* In the new MLA style (2021), we no longer need to indicate the source as "print."

5. *Remove the reference to the city of publication.* It's no longer required. In the new MLA style (2021), we no longer need to include the city of publication for sources published before 1900.

EXAMPLE 2: CORRECTED MLA WORKS CITED PAGE

Gay, Penny. *As She Likes It: Shakespeare's Unruly Women.* Routledge, 2002.

Hamilton, Sharon. *Shakespeare's Daughters.* McFarland, 2003.

EXAMPLE 3: INCORRECT APA REFERENCES PAGE

References

Wessels, W. (1993). "The Minimum Wage and Tipped Employees." Journal of Labor Research, 14(3), 213–226.

"Raising the minimum wage: The Renewed Debate over Fair Labor Standards." (2013). Congressional Digest, 92(5), 1.

What's wrong with the entries of this References page? The writer must:

1. *Double space within each listing AND* between items in the list.
2. *Alphabetize* the list by authors' last names; if the entry has no listed author; simply alphabetize by the first letter of the entry.
3. *Indent second lines* of citations by .5 inches. (Hit the "tab" key.)
4. *Fix the capitalization within the titles. Only* capitalize the first word of the title and proper nouns within the title.
5. *Remove the quotation marks around the titles* of the articles, since the student is using APA Style. (If we were using MLA Style, we'd keep the quotation marks.)

EXAMPLE 4: CORRECTED APA REFERENCES PAGE

References

Raising the minimum wage: The renewed debate over fair labor standards. (2013). *Congressional Digest*, 92(5), 1.

Wessels, W. (1993). The minimum wage and tipped employees. *Journal of Labor Research*, 14(3), 213–226.

For further examples, see the most updated MLA and APA handbooks...

⊷ PART III ⊷
POLISHING YOUR

ESSAY

CHAPTER 8

Revising and Editing Your Essay

All successful writers must learn to edit and revise their work. However, a fine line exists between polishing a paper and editing it to death. No essay is perfect, but with some subtle editing and revising tips, the revision process will help you vastly improve the quality of your work—and your scores.

Typically the mistake beginning writers make is that they attempt to perform *both* the revision and editing processes on their paper simultaneously. Most students who attempt to do both at the same time become frustrated and overwhelmed by the number of issues they must fix. They either give up entirely, or they quickly fix a few issues and leave the rest, hoping the instructor won't notice. Neither strategy is a good one. *It's best to treat revising and editing as two distinct and separate processes.*

Separating the editing and revising processes will help reduce your stress while writing and improve the quality of your work. At this point, you may be asking what, exactly, is the difference between revising and editing?

REVISING: Making substantial, in-depth changes to the essay's ideas, structure, or purpose. This step may include:

- Adding an entire new paragraph
- Removing weak paragraphs
- Inserting opposing viewpoints and evidence to point out their flaws
- Introducing new research

EDITING: Fixing surface errors in organization, grammar, spelling, and punctuation. This step may include:

- Deleting words or sentences to fix awkward or vague phrasing
- Altering the order of paragraphs
- Changing or adding formats or fonts
- Correcting spelling or citations

BEYOND THE CLASSROOM

Most job seekers immediately understand the value of revising their résumé, cover letter, and any other documents needed to secure a great new position. However, even after you attain the job you worked so hard to acquire, you will want to keep it, and revising your work is critical to doing so.

You might be surprised to learn how many employees send out e-mails to their colleagues or clients without proper punctuation, capitalization, and word choice. Although occasional typos and grammar errors do occur, if your written work is rife with errors and smacks of lazy revision skills, your chances of getting a promotion will be slim to none.

Employers value employees who communicate well and essentially make them and the company or organization look good. Most communication in the workplace is written—such as e-mails, webinars, memos, press releases, briefs, project proposals, and policy statements. Your future job will likely require you to create and/or respond to these types of documents regularly, and your ability to do so may mean the difference between receiving a promotion or not. If you invest in your writing abilities now, you'll be able to easily tackle this type of work later, and you'll realize the investment you made in your writing skills has paid off beyond the college classroom.

REVISING STRATEGIES

Most writers begin with the revising process since it is more extensive and involved. To get the most out of revision, consider using one or several of these strategies:

1. **PLAY DEVIL'S ADVOCATE.** Imagine a hostile reader who wishes to discredit all of your points and examples.

   - **Identify potential points of attack.** Determine how to strengthen these areas. Then, ask yourself: Why did you include them at all? How do your examples work to defend and explain your claims? Record your answers to these questions, and save them for the revision process. (You can either do this exercise aloud and then write down your responses or complete it entirely in writing. Try both methods, and see which you prefer.)

   - **Consider opposing viewpoints.** For example, if you argue *for* raising the federal minimum wage for tipped employees in your essay, then you should spend ample time brainstorming reasons *against* raising it. (If you cannot think of any reasons yourself, research what arguments opponents have advanced.) Once you have a handle on the key opposing arguments, you can better address why you feel these arguments lack logic or value and can then point out these flaws in your work.

2. **CONSIDER YOUR AUDIENCE.** An eloquent, thorough argument unfortunately does not guarantee audience persuasion. To ensure you reach and convince your audience, ask yourself, "Who will read my work?" For most collegiate essays, the audience is the professor; however, also consider the larger audience for the topic. If you write about legalization of abortion, for example, to whom would you address this essay? Doctors? State agencies? Patients? Parents of pregnant teenagers? All voters? If the assignment is not this spe-

cific, request permission to write for a specific audience; having a defined audience allows you (as a writer) to better focus your points and examples and also helps you better control the topic.

3. **DISCUSS YOUR IDEAS WITH OTHERS.** Ask a friend, family member, or instructor to listen to your ideas, and encourage them to ask you as many questions as possible about the topic—the more difficult and probing, the better. The more you explain your ideas to others and are forced to answer questions and defend your stances, the better your command of the topic's key talking points will become—and the more sophisticated your thoughts on them will be.

This sample revision process, completed by Russell as he worked on his minimum wage essay, employs part of strategy #1 (considering opposing viewpoints). His process, outlined below, represents only a sample of one way to revise an essay. Every writer's process varies, so feel free to apply the strategies to best suit your process.

1. OPPONENTS SAY:
Waiting on tables, making drinks, and cooking food aren't highly skilled jobs. If these people want to make lots of money, they should go to college and learn a "real" skill.

MY REBUTTAL:
First, asking for a livable wage that amounts to just half of the federal minimum isn't asking for "lots of money"; it's asking for just that: a livable wage that lets these workers have food, shelter, transportation, and access to education. It also helps them get out and spend so the economy stays strong. Second, how are they supposed to go out and learn these so-called "real" skills if they have to work 60 hours a week just to pay the rent? Go to college? Are you kidding? Have these guys actually looked at tuition prices, especially for the top colleges that teach "real"

skills that lead to "lots of money"?? Even public colleges are raising tuition let alone the Ivy League ones. Third, as Allegretto and Cooper (2014) show, there are approximately 4.3 million tipped workers in the United States, and 46% of them have to go get on public assistance—that means WE are subsidizing their pay so restaurant owners don't have to, and that's ridiculous. Lastly, Allegretto and Cooper say this isn't just about tipped employees. Low wage floors "exacerbate the general stagnation of wages for the vast majority of American workers."

2. OPPONENTS SAY:

Restaurants don't want to pay workers more, so they'll just lay them off, which will hurt the very workers the increase is designed to help, and it'll harm the economy.

MY REBUTTAL:

Hmmm. Restaurant owners do seem pretty greedy, so these people may have a point here. I guess I need to see if I can find some economists or other experts who say that this is not true. Wouldn't giving these workers more money actually help the economy? The more money they have, the more they have to spend, which creates more jobs and circulates to other people and businesses, doesn't it?

In completing this strategy, Russell realized he did not have a clear rebuttal for his second opposition statement concerning the connection between minimum wage rates and economic health. However, this realization led to *finding* an answer which, in turn, led to a stronger, more convincing argument in the final draft.

Read Russell's first draft paragraph below and see what you think...

RUSSELL'S ORIGINAL PARAGRAPH:

People who say Increasing the federal minimum wage for tipped employees won't help stimulate our economy are idiots. Are they serious?? Increased wages obviously mean increased spending and circulation of money, which leads to economic growth. According to Sylvia Allegretto and David Cooper (2014) of The Economic Policy Institute, we have 4.3 million tipped restaurant employees in the United States (p. 7). Giving over four million people more money to spend each month would make a huge difference in our economy. Raising their wage to be half the federal minimum wage (currently set at $7.25/hour) would mean raising it to just $3.63 per hour. This raise may not sound like much, but it would give workers an extra $1.50 to spend for every hour they work. Multiply this $1.50 times the number of hours worked by every tipped employee in the entire country, and exponentially we increase the circulation of money in our economy. For example, if all tipped employees only worked twenty hours per week for fifty weeks per year, that would mean they have an additional $1,500 each to spend in our economy that year. Multiply this $1,500 by the estimated four million tipped restaurant employees, and we would see an extra $6,000,000,000 (six *billion* dollars) distributed into our economy *each year*. How could anyone argue that raising the minimum wage is anything but wise?

Russell's getting there, isn't he? He's cited evidence to support his point, and he also explains and expounds upon that evidence. Yet, after a peer reads this paragraph and notes the tone sounds rather insulting, Russell begins to revise. He's careful to avoid insults and instead focuses on presenting the opposing view and explaining why, based on his research, he sees this view as invalid.

He also realizes he ended the paragraph with a question instead of a statement, so he tries a more sophisticated strategy. Rather than posing the question and just hoping readers answer it as he wishes, he *answers* that question clearly.

This is indeed a much more effective strategy because it allows Russell to *tell* and *show* readers why the opposing view is invalid rather than assuming they understand or agree.

See Russell's revised paragraph below:

RUSSELL'S REVISED PARAGRAPH

Opponents to raising the federal tipped employee minimum wage warn that this increase will actually lead to greater unemployment and a damaged economy, but in reality, increasing the federal minimum wage for tipped employees will stimulate our economy. Increased wages will mean increased spending and circulation of money, which leads to economic growth. Economists David Cooper and Doug Hall (2013) found that raising the minimum wage would "provide a modest stimulus to the entire economy, as increased wages would lead to increased consumer spending, which would contribute to GDP growth and modest employment gains" (p. 2). Michael Lynn and Christopher Boone (2015) agree and found that despite wage opponents' dire predictions, raising tipped employees' wages won't cause restaurants to close or lay off people. In fact, their research shows that the increases had "*no* linear effect on the number of full-service restaurants or on full-service restaurant employment, even when looking at cumulative effects over three years" (p. 10). It's hard to ignore this overwhelming evidence, especially when considering that we have roughly four million tipped restaurant employees in the United States (*Allegretto & Cooper, 2014*, p. 7). Giving *four million* people more money to spend each month would make a huge difference in our economy. Raising their wage to half the federal minimum wage (currently set at $7.25/hour) *would mean raising it to just $3.63 per hour. This increase may not sound like much, but it would give workers an extra $1.50 to spend for every hour they work.* Multiply this $1.50 times the number of hours worked by every tipped employee in the entire country, and exponentially we increase the circulation of money in our economy. For example, if all tipped employees only worked twenty hours per week for fifty weeks per year, that would mean they have an additional $1,500 each to spend in our economy that year. Multiply this $1,500 by the estimated four million tipped restaurant employees, and we would see an extra $6,000,000,000 (six *billion* dollars) distributed into our economy *each year*. With all this money, we can improve local businesses and communities; have a better, stronger economy; and rely on less federal spending—meaning our taxes will be lower.

CONTROLLING THE CRITIC

With all this talk of revising, many students often get nervous. It is usually at this point in the writing process that the voice of The Critic becomes unbearable. Some students are not sure when to stop revising, and some inner critics are so brutal in their commentary that students worry how they can listen to The Critic without feeling beat up and frustrated afterward.

The Critic typically has much to say about our work, but how can we know which of these scathing criticisms we should accept and fix and which we should ignore or alter? Listen only to constructive, helpful criticism—not mean-spirited, judgmental criticism.

Helpful criticism is not necessarily always positive, but it is always *constructive*, meaning that it gives the writer direction. It indicates how to go about fixing the problem(s) identified. Judgmental criticism, on the other hand, shuts down conversation and merely insults the writer. It rarely offers any direction for future composition.

Consider the following issue Jenny experienced while writing a comparison/contrast analysis essay on two male characters, Peter Griffin from *Family Guy* and Homer Simpson from *The Simpsons*. She wrote the following ideas on the topic.

> Peter and Homer are a lot alike, but they are also different. It seems like Homer is like a good guy on the inside and means well even though he definitely does stupid things. Peter is an idiot, too, but he is more of a mean idiot. He doesn't seem to care about anyone but himself. Even his kids are secondary. Both guys have the whole house and three kids plus two cars and all that. But when you watch the show, you realize Homer actually cares about his family but Peter doesn't. What is this saying to viewers? Are they making fun of Homer and Peter, or are they saying this is good?

Her inner Critic then blasted the work with the following criticisms.

> "This is so lame. What is this? I haven't even said anything."

> "I'm a terrible writer. I hate writing. I never know what to say. I don't know how to make this sound right. I'm just not good at English."

Clearly, Jenny's inner Critic is busily ripping her work, and her self-esteem, to shreds. Should she listen? Did The Critic offer her helpful, constructive direction with which she could improve her writing?

This Critic's judgment is *de*structive, not *con*structive. Jenny understandably felt frustrated and ready to quit. However, once she probed further into the criticism—while avoiding the judgment statements— she realized how to fix the issues she saw in her writing. In the example below, Jenny tackled each of The Critic's judgments and replaced it with a constructive criticism.

> **JUDGMENT:** "This is so lame."
>
> **HOW TO FIX IT:** Remove the judgmental term *lame*, and probe deeper to find the nature of the problem.
>
> **CONSTRUCTIVE CRITICISM:** What exactly is the problem with the information? Is it too vague? If so, which specific elements or details in the paragraph are unclear?

> **JUDGMENT:** "What is this? I haven't even said anything."
>
> **HOW TO FIX IT:** Specify these questions to elicit definitive answers.
>
> **CONSTRUCTIVE CRITICISM:** What is "what"? Define "this." Do you mean that the point of the paragraph is unclear? What is it you want to say, exactly?

> **JUDGMENT:** "I'm a terrible writer. I hate writing. I never know what to say. I don't know how to make this sound right. I'm just not good at English."
>
> **HOW TO FIX IT:** Remove the judgment about whether you are a "good" writer, and throw out the verdict of your per-

ceived abilities in English. Don't turn one perceived problem with one paragraph on one paper in one class into an overall indication of your abilities in an entire discipline. **CONSTRUCTIVE CRITICISM:** What exactly is "terrible" about the paragraph? Is the information inaccurate? Does it need more supporting evidence? What do you mean by "sound right"? Is the writing grammatically incorrect, or do you mean the tone needs to be more formal?

Struggling with writing is *not* an indication of lack of talent or ability; it just goes with the territory of creating. *All* writers and artists struggle, and no matter how great a writer you become, you will struggle at times. Use these struggles to learn more about your strengths and weaknesses so you can continuously improve.

PEER REVIEW

Yet another way to improve and polish your work is to participate in a writing exercise called *peer review*.

Peer review is exactly what it sounds like: It's an activity in which you review your peers' work—and your peers review yours.

If peer review is required in your college writing classes (and it most likely *will* be), you may be wondering: How might a writer get the most out of peer review?

1. CONSIDER YOUR PEERS' ADVICE—BUT DON'T NECESSARILY TAKE IT.

Some of your fellow students may be geniuses whose every suggestion should be taken as gospel, but others . . . perhaps not. Part of your job as a writer is to know what advice to take—and not take.

How can you tell?

Once you get your review back, *read over your peers' notes*. Write down or circle any notes that echo with truth or insight. Put a question mark next to any notes you either didn't understand or don't necessarily agree with completely. If you can ask follow-up questions to the reviewer, then do so.

Then, *let the comments and feedback sit for a few hours*, even a full day, then reread them.

Ask yourself if the comments are

- Accurate?
- Insightful?
- Helpful?

If so, follow the reviewer's sage advice. If not, *figure out why not*. If the reviewers' comments anger or frustrate you at first, put them aside for a day or two, or if you don't have that much time, perhaps an hour or two. Then, return to them and try to be open to hearing the *spirit* of what the reviewer meant.

Often, when we calm down and truly listen, we gain the discernment to realize whether the reviewer was correct or not. If yes, then we can set to work on fixing the issues. If they were *not* correct, the good news is that you can still benefit from their notes. How?

ASK YOURSELF:

- What did the reviewer not quite understand about your work?
  - Was the thesis unclear?
  - Perhaps the significance of your evidence was not fully explained?
  - Are you missing defined topic sentences in each body paragraph?
- How might you remove any lack of clarity the reviewer experienced in your current draft?
  - Rework the organization?
  - Add more evidence?
  - Rephrase key explanation sentences?

Even if you ultimately discard your peers' feedback because it's entirely off base, the very fact of mulling over notes and weighing their value makes you a better, smarter writer.

How?

Getting others' perspectives on your writing deepens your understanding of how others perceive your writing. You'll thus gain insight into how you might improve and the ways in which you can reach readers on a deeper level. All of this consideration leads to richer, more powerful writing.

Yet, at the end of the day, remember that it's *your* name going on that essay and *your* grade on the line. So, if you simply do not agree with your peers' feedback, that's perfectly okay. You're the author, so it's *your* choice.

2. DON'T BE OVERLY SENSITIVE OR "PRECIOUS" WITH YOUR WORK.

Editors and readers will almost *always* find something they either don't like or don't understand about our work. That's okay. It happens to even the best writers.

So, when this happens to you, don't panic, or worse, tear into your peer and accuse them of idiocy simply because they didn't like or appreciate your work.

Being a writer means being edited and critiqued, so don't take commentaries on your work personally!

Be open to genuine, constructive feedback, even if it's suggestions for improvement. We can all always improve . . .

The only exception here would be abusive, mean-spirited feedback that bullies or belittles you. If that's the case, then speak to the reviewer to let them know their comments are unhelpful, hurtful, and/or even destructive. (Sometimes, reviewers are unaware how their feedback is perceived.) Yet, if the person refuses to change or even hear you, then you'll likely need to go to your instructor.

3. BE A GREAT PEER REVIEWER YOURSELF.

We'll discuss this point in depth shortly, but for now, keep in mind that the more attention and effort you put into reading and editing *others' work*, the more adept you become at editing *your own*. Switching from reader to writer is difficult, but the more you practice doing just that, the better you'll become at it, and soon your editing eye will be so honed that you'll become your own best editor.

Besides, by reading a fellow writer's work, we see how *they* developed and explained their ideas; we learn how *they* organized their points and what sources *they* cited to defend their position. We can also clearly see the places where their strategies didn't quite pay off, and in seeing those mistakes, we can avoid them in our work.

In other words, reading the work of other writers absolutely can and does inspire and improve our own. So, let's now discuss more specific strategies you can employ to become a great peer reviewer.

HOW TO BE A GREAT PEER REVIEWER

1. *REVIEW* YOUR PEERS' WORK; DON'T MERELY *ASSESS* IT

To *assess* someone's work is to give an overall appraisal, such as "excellent," "good," "average," or "poor," etc.

To *review* someone's work is to give an in-depth analysis and evaluation of the work, with examples and comprehensive notes.

Consider, for example, the following two comments. Imagine two of your peers offered you this feedback on your essay. Did your peers offer a *review* of your work, or merely an *assessment*?

- Peer #1's Feedback: "Good job."
- Peer #2's Feedback: "I found it kinda confusing."

If you said the peers simply assessed your work, you're correct. To review it, they should tell you WHAT was good exactly or WHICH SPECIFIC ASPECTS confused them.

In other words, when reviewing your peers' work, *avoid vague generalities* that give no room for improvement or clear direction on how to revise. It's fine to offer an overall *assessment* (such as, "This essay is great!" or "This essay needs further development"), but don't stop there.

Tell the writer what *specific* aspects of the essay were "great" or "need further development," etc.—and why.

At first, most writers love the positive assessment of "good job," but once we have a moment to think about it, we'll realize it wasn't all that helpful after all. Why not? It gives us *zero* direction for improvement. What *exactly* about the essay was good? Every single element? There is absolutely nothing whatsoever that we could improve?!

Clearly, the "I got confused" feedback proves unhelpful as well. Which specific elements did the reviewer find confusing? Where? Why?

Since they did not point to any examples, we have no idea and thus no way to fix the alleged problem(s).

This is why it's so important to be *specific when* you *are the reviewer.* Tell your writers:

- What—specifically—works about the essay?
    - The language/word choice?
    - The overall structure?
    - The thesis?
    - The strength of the argument?
- What—specifically—needs improvement in the essay?
    - The conclusion?
    - The overall structure?
    - The evidence?
    - The tone?

When you're specific and detailed in giving your peers advice, you'll soon be considered a valuable peer reviewer. Your fellow students will likely return the favor, and soon you'll receive better, more defined feedback on *your* work, too.

2. POINT OUT THE GOOD *AND* THE BAD

Many people think giving feedback means pointing out everything that they don't like or found "wrong" with someone else's work. It does not.

Reviewing the work of another writer means evaluating its strengths *and* weaknesses. It means offering insight into its merits and flaws.

So, tell your peers what works and what does not work

so they can learn from BOTH their strengths and their weaknesses.

Besides, if you only point out what's wrong, they probably won't hear you, anyway, and you may get a reputation for being a "bad" reviewer, even if all your negative feedback is technically accurate. The same is true for strictly positive feedback. There's always *some* aspect of our work we can improve, so even if the essay is absolutely stellar, do your best to find something the writer could make even stronger.

3. BE HONEST BUT DO *NOT* BE BRUTAL

This point is probably the most important because often students feel awkward pointing out other writers' mistakes. However, finding both the pros and cons of the writing is part of your job as the reviewer. If the essay is disorganized and unclear, don't tell the writer it's "good" to spare their feelings. You're not doing your peer a favor by lying!

However, there's also no need to be brutal. If you read a paper that in your opinion is terrible, do NOT tell the writer, "Hey, your essay is AWFUL!"

Instead, kindly identify what particular problems you see—and offer suggestions for improvement.

For example, if you cannot clearly identify the thesis, then say so. If the body paragraphs do not use the P.I.E. (Point, Illustrate, Explain) format, so you found them difficult to follow, point out this fact. Then, if you have suggestions on how to fix, share!

YOU MIGHT ALSO TRY THE CLASSIC "COMPLIMENT SANDWICH"

1. COMPLIMENT

Start your comments with positive feedback—elements you liked or felt really worked well. (Remember, be genuine here!)

2. PROBLEMS/ISSUES/OPPORTUNITIES

Then, offer constructive or "opportunity" feedback—aspects of the essay that aren't quite working yet. (Don't be brutal, though!)

3. COMPLIMENT

Finally, conclude with a final compliment or note of encouragement.

When you sandwich the so-called negative comments between complimentary ones, most writers will be more open to hearing your feedback. (Aren't *you* more open to others' feedback when they start and end with compliments?!)

To help us practice, let's take a look at a few quick examples of peer reviews so you can see the difference between helpful and not-so-helpful feedback . . .

PEER REVIEW EXAMPLES

Below you will find three peer review examples. Read them and imagine they were *your* peers giving *you* feedback. Which is the most helpful? Why? How might you apply what you learned here to your own peer reviewing in class?

PEER REVIEW #1

Good job. I liked it. It was impressive!

PEER REVIEW #2

Um . . . IDK. I didn't really follow your points too well. Could you be more specific on stuff?

PEER REVIEW #3

Nice job on the thesis. I knew your position instantly, and I could tell what each of your body paragraph's topics were, so there were no surprises when reading the actual essay. Your topic sentences were super clear and well worded, and they matched the thesis. Nice!

Man, you nailed it in body paragraphs 1 and 2. I was with you the whole time 'cause you followed P.I.E. Your evidence was super clear and you explained it great so I could envision what you were saying, like about the whole suicide thing and how it related to the rottenness in the play and even the idea of revenge. You kinda made me rethink my argument about the overall theme of the play!

In BP3, I got confused 'cause I felt like this was another body paragraph, but then the essay just stopped after that. I wasn't sure if you just forgot the conclusion or if this paragraph WAS the conclusion?

Grammar and spelling were good, except for a few comma issues that I circled.

Overall, I think you've done a good job so far!

Initially, we may like the simplicity of the comments by the first "reviewer" (especially since they are complimentary!), but in actuality they provide us merely with an overall assessment of the essay—not a review. They tell us nothing about which specific aspects worked and how or why, and no suggestions whatsoever are offered in terms of opportunities to improve or expand. Is the reviewer suggesting there is zero room for improvement?! Clearly, that's not the case. We can *always* improve!

The second "reviewer," too, has offered us virtually nothing because instead of reviewing our work, they merely assessed it. They state that we need to be "more specific on stuff"? What "stuff"? Where? How? In a three-page essay, they could not find *one example* to offer?? This reviewer should follow their own advice and be more specific in their comments!

Clearly, in the long run, the third peer reviewer's work will help us the most. It gives us *specific*, direction-based feedback. We know what specific aspects of the essay worked and which did not (in their opinion). We can disagree with their feedback, of course, but at least now we have some clear suggestions to consider, rather than vague generalities that get us nowhere.

EDITING

Use the following strategies to help edit your work. Remember, editing is a surface-level task, which means you will focus on word choice, grammar, spelling, and punctuation.

- **READ YOUR WORK ALOUD.** The sound of your ideas and language (whether good or not) will come across, and any awkward sentences will be easy to fix once you hear them. Ensure your tone and word choice are formal enough for an academic audience. (Further information on word choice can be found later in this chapter).

- **READ THE ESSAY BACKWARD.** Check your essay for errors by combing through it from end to beginning; start at the end and read the last sentence, then the penultimate sentence, and so on as you move toward the first word. Don't read for content; search only for grammar, spelling, and punctuation errors. Reading backward allows you to look at your paper as simply a collection of sentences so you can avoid getting caught up in the ideas or arguments presented.

- **GET ANOTHER PAIR OF EYES ON THE PAPER.** Take advantage of your college's Writing Center or Learning Lab, both of which often offer free writing assistance to registered students, or ask a trusted, intelligent friend or family member to look it over for you.

- **TAKE BREAKS.** Our minds grow tired of working on the same task for long periods of time. So write for a while, but don't be afraid to take breaks. Return to the paper when your mind has had a chance to process and rest. Most writing instructors recommend writing an essay over a period of three to four days. (If the essay is more than ten pages long, you will likely need four to five days.)

- **READ THE ESSAY BOTH ON THE SCREEN AND IN PRINT.** Our eyes can often play tricks on us when we read. Some people can catch errors on a screen that they would miss in print and vice versa, so before you turn in the final draft, print it and read the hard copy. Also read it on the computer screen. Using both methods will ensure the best results.
- **GO TO OFFICE HOURS.** Office hours give you the opportunity to seek help from the very person who will grade your essay: your instructor. So scope out the instructor's office, and stop by with your paper in tow. Chances are you'll be glad you did; most instructors see office visits as a compliment, and they are happy to help their students succeed. Even if the visit doesn't prove as helpful as you hoped, what have you lost? Fifteen minutes? It's common for a student to go over her essay with her instructor and raise her essay score by an entire letter grade. Gambling fifteen minutes to potentially gain such a vast improvement in your grade is definitely a low-risk investment.

See the pages that follow for examples of editing for specific errors (such as word choice, commas, semicolons, apostrophes, etc.).

WORD CHOICE

The use of language within any written work largely determines how readers perceive both it and its writer. As arguably the greatest writer of the English language, William Shakespeare achieved unsurpassed brilliance in language. His works remain known, read, and celebrated all over the world—and scholars often refer both to his work and to *him* as preeminent.

How did Shakespeare achieve such an impressive feat with his writing? Different scholars attribute his successes differently, but his mastery of language is irrefutable and clearly stands at the center of his eminent success.

> Just as sculptors use clay, wax, metal, and other materials to bring their visions to life for viewers, writers use **words** to bring their ideas and analyses to life for readers.

Fear not; professors certainly don't expect their students to turn in masterpieces that rival the genius of Shakespeare! However, they *do* expect their students to consider word choice in their essays and to effectively convey meaning through the phrasing they select.

Consider the examples below that theoretically convey similar meanings, and decide which you feel speaks to the audience most effectively.

EXAMPLE 1:

A. Cowards end up feeling really depressed because every time they have the chance to do something great, they don't do it, so they feel so bad that it's almost like they die a little every time they don't live up to their potential. It's like they are dead while they are really alive. On the other hand, people who are brave and take risks don't have to go through all these little deaths while they are living. They will only have to die when they actually die.

B. Cowards die many times before their deaths; the valiant never taste of death but once (*Julius Caesar* II, ii, 32-4).

EXAMPLE 2:

A. I wonder if death would be an improvement to this crappy, meaningless life; I mean, what's the point of living? What are we doing here?

B. To be or not to be; that is the question (*Hamlet* III, i, 57).

EXAMPLE 3:

A. There were many bad things happening at that time, but then there were also good things happening, so it was like that time in our lives was both good and bad, bitter and sweet.

B. It was the best of times; it was the worst of times ... (Dickens 1).

Most readers select choice B as the more eloquently written phrasing in each of the above examples. Why? Although different readers prefer different writing styles, the word choice and structure of sentence B in each example succinctly, clearly, and directly imparts meaning to the reader. Perhaps this clarity points to the reason these quotes have gained such notoriety over time. (Examples 1 and 2 are from Shakespeare—*Julius Caesar* and *Hamlet* respectively; Example 3 is from Charles Dickens's *A Tale of Two Cities*).

> Although using precise wording is not easy, when you take the time to ensure your language and structure convey precisely what you mean, your instructor will likely reward you with the high score you deserve.

Again, don't feel your professors expect your writing to rival the mastery of Shakespeare or Dickens. Yet, by all means, strive to elevate your vocabulary and writing style. Here are a few ways to approach it:

- Invest in a quality dictionary and thesaurus, or, at the very least, consult online dictionaries and thesauri. (Use *The Oxford English Dictionary*; most professors consider it the best.)
- Use precise, formal language—avoid slang and informal phrasing.
- Use the proper forms of words; especially check for commonly misspelled words and phrases.
- Read, read, read—the more you read, the better and more quickly your brain will process language and structure.
- Write, write, write—as with anything else, the more you practice a skill, the better you will become at it.

BANNED WORDS AND PHRASES

Avoid using the following words and phrases in academic writing to help formalize your tone, specify your language, and improve reader understanding. The chart below contains explanations of:

1. Why writers should avoid each term or phrase
2. Suggestions for alternatives

BANNED WORD/ PHRASE	WHY?	USE INSTEAD
• today • today's world • today's society • the world • society • nowadays • currently	These vague, unclear terms lead to confusion for readers. (What does the writer mean by "today" or "nowadays"? Within the last ten years? Fifty years? One hundred years? This language also points to concepts entirely too large to adequately discuss in a 7–10 page paper. Instead, name the specific time period or group to which you refer.	• Contemporary society • Twenty-first-century society • Twentieth-century society • Contemporary American society • Contemporary Western society • Western industrialized societies
• kind of • sort of	These words are vague and too informal for an academic essay.	• slightly • somewhat • relatively • merely • simply
• y'all • ain't • can't • don't • wouldn't, etc.	Avoid using contractions and informal language in an academic paper. Spell out contractions, and formalize word choice.	• cannot • do not • would not, etc. (Use neither "y'all" nor "you all" in academic writing; both are too informal.)

BANNED WORD/ PHRASE	WHY?	USE INSTEAD
• this • that (without a clear modifier)	Use a clear modifier to define this pronoun reference—usually inserting a noun will fix the problem.	• this *quote* • this *idea* • this *point* • that *statement* • that *notion* • that *claim*
• studies show • research indicates • studies prove	These words indicate vague, unclear source citation—*never* refer to research or facts in an abstract manner. Cite only specific information from a known, credible source as evidence. Refer to a specific study, scholar, or finding—and cite your source.	• A 2007 Harvard Medical School survey reveals ... • NASA scientist John Smith claims ... • The 2010 U.S. Census shows ... • Renowned fairy tale scholar Jack Zipes argues ...
• really • totally	Formalize this language.	• wholly • utterly • entirely • purely
• you • your • yours	Directly addressing the reader works only in limited scenarios, so unless you have an excellent reason to use second-person pronouns, replace them in academic essays.	Ask yourself to whom you refer when writing "you." Most likely, you mean: • one • readers • viewers • scholars

BANNED WORD/ PHRASE	WHY?	USE INSTEAD
• I • me • my • mine	In most cases, the use of the word *I* is both distracting and unnecessary. Since writers include their names on the title page as the author, readers understand everything included represents the writer's opinion. To state "I think" throughout an essay is not necessary—and it weakens the argument by drawing attention to each idea's status as a mere opinion.	Achieve greater persuasive power by simply eliminating *I* and its verb. **EXAMPLE:** "I think the writer conveys the inner strength of the character through her lack of dialogue." Simply cut out "I think" to revise the sentence: "The writer conveys the inner strength of the character through her lack of dialogue."
Slang and informal language, such as: • cool • awesome • busted • bummer • dude • hick • flaky • cheesy	Writing formal papers for a college or university class requires using formal language that conveys professionalism and credibility; the terms listed in the prior column will achieve the opposite effect.	Use a dictionary or thesaurus to replace informal language with more specialized, specific, and formal phrasing.
for all intents and purposes	Clunky, awkward, and unnecessary	because
• due to the fact that • on account of • in order to	Wordy and unnecessary	• because • since • to

INCLUSIVE LANGUAGE

Few writers strive to upset, offend, or anger readers—especially when writing for a grade. Yet, sometimes we do exactly that by unknowingly using biased, outdated language that excludes or insults our readers.

For this reason, it's critical we purposefully choose respectful, inclusive language free of words, phrases, or tones that insult, demean, or devalue other human beings.

Granted, learning to write inclusively can be a challenge at first, especially if we have not been asked to do so in the past. However, with practice and proper care and research, we can soon master the art of writing with inclusion.

To begin, let's first define what "inclusive language" *is*, exactly, and then we'll go over some general guiding principles as well as some examples.

WHAT IS "INCLUSIVE LANGUAGE"?

Inclusive language is *not* about being "politically correct" or "pandering" to this group or that one—it is simply about honoring our readers, no matter who or where they are. When we honor readers, our readers will honor us, whether that's via high grades, publication, stellar reviews, or book sales, etc. . . .

To ensure you achieve this honor in your work, simply follow the principles outlined below, and see the MLA or APA handbooks for further advice.

You can also visit your instructor's office hours and/or your school's learning lab or writing center for assistance with using inclusive, respectful language.

INCLUSIVE WRITING RULE #1: REMOVE IRRELEVANT REFERENCES TO A PERSON'S IDENTITY

Examples of "identity" references include allusions to a person's

- Gender
- Race
- Ethnicity
- Age
- Religion
- Sexual orientation
- Marital status
- Disability
- Social or economic status
- Political affiliation

Although at times these references can be quite meaningful in the context of a discussion, usually they are not. So, you'll need to use your best judgment when including them, and if you can't justify their inclusion in the conversation or argument, simply eliminate them entirely.

We'll go over examples below to help illustrate how, when, and why you might either include or omit such references. These examples will hopefully inspire you with ideas on ways to achieve greater honor and precision in your language, but . . .

Don't try to simply memorize any particular phrasing.

Cultures shift and change frequently, often in the blink of an eye, so words and phrases considered "inclusive" today could be outdated tomorrow!

Thus, instead of memorizing the language in this section, focus on the *spirit* of inclusiveness. This way, you can fashion your own phraseology that honors your readers, feels comfortable for you, and is most current.

Let's take a look at a few examples . . .

EXAMPLE 1

NO: The <u>female</u> district attorney argued the case passionately.

YES: The district attorney argued the case passionately.

WHY: Drop unnecessary gender references—unless, for some reason, they are relevant. Then, clearly address the significance of gender so it's clear why you're mentioning it. In this case, why does it matter that the attorney is female? It likely does not, so drop the reference.

EXAMPLE 2

NO: We must achieve this goal for all <u>man</u>kind.

YES: We must achieve this goal for all humankind.

WHY: Avoid using "man" or "men" as a stand-in for humans or human beings. All humans are clearly not male, so unless you literally are referring to a human male or group of males, then simply use "human," "humans," "humankind," "individuals" or "people," etc., depending on the context.

EXAMPLE 3

NO: John Manes, an <u>African American</u> U.S. senator, will speak this afternoon in the quad regarding the proposed tuition increase.

YES: John Manes, a U.S. senator, will speak this afternoon in the quad regarding the proposed tuition increase.

WHY: Do NOT refer to a person's race unless it is critical to the conversation, and if you do mention a person's race, make clear why that identity is significant within the context of your discussion. In this case, it's likely not, so drop it.

In the above examples, references to the individuals' identities proved irrelevant to (and likely distracting from) the overall discussion. However, if you're thinking that, at times, noting a person's identity *can* be an important, vital aspect of a conversation, you're correct.

The question is: How can you distinguish when this information is needed . . . or not? When considering including an individual's identity, ask yourself this question:

WHAT DOES SUCH INCLUSION ACCOMPLISH?

If you do *not* have an excellent answer to this question, then either

1. Find an answer

   OR

2. Remove the reference to identity completely.

If you do come up with an excellent answer, *include this answer in your discussion*. This way, readers clearly understand *why* you're mentioning the individual's race, gender, age, or socioeconomic status, etc. Don't assume the significance is obvious. It might be obvious to you, perhaps, but it likely is not to readers, so be sure and explain it.

Read the following examples and see if you feel it might be appropriate to mention the person's race, gender, or ethnicity, etc.

EXAMPLE 1

> Richard Theodore Greener graduated from Harvard College in 1870 as the first Black graduate in the college's history. He went on to become a professor, lawyer, and diplomat, and eventually the dean of the Howard University School of Law. To achieve such heights as a person of color in the era in which Greener achieved them is not only impressive but also inspiring.

Including a reference to Greener's race in this example works well because it illustrates the impressive nature of his credentials. For a person of color to graduate from the oldest and arguably most illustrious university in the United States in 1870—just five years after the end of the

American Civil War—is indeed extraordinary, even inspiring, as the writer rightly points out.

EXAMPLE 2

> Many enterprising and talented women are often over-looked in male-dominated aerospace and aviation text-books. Take, for example, Lilian Bland. Bland was the first woman to design, build, and fly an aircraft. Consider, too, Harriet Quimby, the first woman to fly across the English Channel. Next is Marie Marvingt, the first woman to fly a fighter plane in combat.

Since this writer is discussing the lack of female inclusion in male-dominated aviation texts, stressing the gender of the accomplished aviators is not only acceptable but crucial to the discussion.

EXAMPLE 3

> As a low-income, first-generation college student, I know firsthand how difficult it is to gain access to a college edu-cation, particularly for people in low-income communities.

Although in general we want to be careful with using the word "I" in our academic writing, in this particular case, the student is tapping into their own experience to highlight their expertise within and knowledge about their topic. So long as the professor approves the use of first-person in the essay, then the student citing their own background and experience is not only appropriate but highly effective.

INCLUSIVE WRITING RULE #2: USE PEOPLE-FIRST LANGUAGE

When writing or speaking of others, use terminology that *focuses on the person first*, rather than on a method of categorization.

To speak first of a person's "category" and then of the human can come across as dehumanizing, and it may alienate your readers or audience. Instead, prioritize *personhood* over *identity*.

EXAMPLE 1:

> <u>NO</u>: A Down syndrome person
> <u>YES</u>: A person with Down syndrome

EXAMPLE 2:

> <u>NO</u>: A homeless person
> <u>YES</u>: A person experiencing homelessness

EXAMPLE 3:

> <u>NO</u>: Foster children or foster youth
> <u>YES</u>: Children or youth in foster care

EXAMPLE 4:

> <u>NO</u>: Abused or neglected teens
> <u>YES</u>: Teens who experienced abuse or neglect

EXAMPLE 5:

> <u>NO</u>: High-risk students
> <u>YES</u>: Students at high risk

CAUTION: EXCEPTION!

Members of a few groups feel quite proud of their identities and wish to have those identities listed *first*.

For example, many deaf and autistic people prefer *identity-first language* because, to them, being deaf or autistic is a critical part of their identity. They do *not* see deafness or autism as a "deficit," and they wish to remind others of this fact. Thus, they may prefer using the phrase "a deaf person" to "a person who is deaf" or "an autistic person" rather than "a person with autism."

However, these references can vary from person to person (and thus become difficult to remember!), so check with the particular person or group about whom you're writing and use the language or phraseology *they* recommend. You can also check an updated dictionary or ask your instructor.

INCLUSIVE WRITING RULE #3: AVOID TERMS THAT IMPLY INFERIORITY OR SUPERIORITY

Replace any language that might imply inferiority or superiority of one group or person over another.

Be careful here!

Some terms' implied inferiority is so subtle and the term so widely used that, at first glance, we may not even notice its bias. Yet, upon closer inspection, we can indeed see the language does infer either inferiority or superiority.

EXAMPLE 1:

NO: Minority/Minorities
YES: Historically marginalized population; communities of color; marginalized communities

EXAMPLE 2:

NO: Low-class
YES: Low socioeconomic status

EXAMPLE 3:

NO: A normal person
YES: A person without a disability

EXAMPLE 4

NO: A crazy person; a nut; a psycho, a maniac

> YES: A person with an emotional or behavioral disability, a psychiatric disability, or a mental health impairment

INCLUSIVE WRITING RULE #4: USE ONLY HONORING, RESPECTFUL—AND THE MOST UP-TO-DATE— TERMINOLOGY WHEN REFERRING TO INDIVIDUALS' AGES

Many of the courses you take in college (especially in the social sciences) will likely require writing about individuals in terms of their ages. For example, you may need to specify the age group of the participants you included in your research study or perhaps that of other researchers' studies.

HOW MIGHT YOU REFER TO PERSONS OF "ADVANCED AGE" WITH RESPECT AND HONOR?

Obviously, terms such as "old man" or "old lady" drip with disrespect and ageism, but often it's difficult to know what particular language we *should* use.

Below you will find some suggested terms, both to potentially use and to avoid!

However, *always double-check with your professor to ensure you're using the most precise, updated, and accurate language.*

YES:

(Probably okay to use these terms, but double-check with your professor)

Older persons
Older patients
Older individuals
Older people
Older adults
Persons sixty-five years and older

NO:

(Do *not* use these terms!)

> the elderly
> senile
> the aged or aging
> old person, old man, old woman

Remember, the above examples represent *suggestions* only! Always check with your professor on the precise vocabulary required, particularly for specialized research. Often, researchers must use specialized industry lingo to ensure the universal understanding of their work.

You can also see the MLA and APA handbooks for more examples and further information.

NOTORIOUS CONFUSABLES

Study the correct use and spelling of each of the following words.

AFFECT/EFFECT

Affect is a verb. (Remember, *affect* begins with *a* and so does *action*.) *Effect* is a noun.

> I hope my speech positively **affects** my audience.

> The **effect** of my speech remains unknown.

There is an exception to this rule: When discussing "effecting change," use *effect* rather than *affect*.

> He hopes to **effect** great change during his presidency.

ITS/IT'S

Its is possessive; *It's* is a contraction of *It is*.

> The book and **its** cover are severely tattered.

> **It's** true that the truth will set you free.

Check your usage of *its* or *it's* by inserting *it is* wherever you write *it's*; if you could correctly apply *it is* in place of *it's*, then you have used the proper form. If not, replace *it's* with *its* and ensure you mean to convey ownership.

THERE/THEIR/THEY'RE

There is a location. *Their* is a possessive noun. *They're* is the contraction of *they are*.

> Over **there** you will see my huge Labrador and his dog-house.

> **Their** house is beautiful.

> **They're** the best friends she ever had.

YOUR/YOU'RE

You're is the contraction of *you are*. *Your* is a possessive noun.

> You're the funniest person I have ever known.
>
> Is that your book?

CONSCIENCE/CONSCIOUS

A *conscience* is an internal voice of morality. To be *conscious* is to be aware.

> I thought about stealing the money, but my conscience bothered me too much to do it; even if I got away with the theft, I would always be conscious of my actions.

ACCESS/EXCESS/ASSESS/EXCEPT

To *access* means to gain entrance or usage. *Excess* is an overabundance or too much. To *assess* means to evaluate. *Except* is another word for "aside from" or "excluding."

> I would love to access the library's files, but my library fines are in excess of the limit.
>
> The instructor must assess the quality of the students' papers.
>
> Everyone is going to the party except Jeff.

ADVISE/ADVICE

Advise is a verb. *Advice* is a noun.

> She advised him on the best restaurants in town; he valued her stellar advice.

ILLUSION/ALLUSION/ELUDE

An *illusion* is a false image or belief. An *allusion* is a reference to another work. To *elude* means to evade capture.

When he traveled through the desert, he often saw the illusion of an oasis, but he never actually found one.

The graduation speaker's allusion to Shakespeare's *The Taming of the Shrew* seemed illogical.

The criminal attempted to elude police capture, but she was finally caught.

ANECDOTE/ANTIDOTE

An *anecdote* is a personal story or note. An *antidote* is a cure for poison or relief for a problem.

Our professor's opening anecdote was quite funny, and we liked the way he related his personal experience to the course material.

We readily welcomed the inspiring movie's message as an antidote for the horrifying and destructive impact of the preceding war film.

ASSURE/INSURE/ENSURE

To *assure* is to promise or to give certainty to another person. To *ensure* is to make certain. When you *insure* something, you secure it with a policy.

He assured me the problem would never recur.

We studied both our notes and our textbook to ensure we understood all the material.

We bought the policy to insure our home against fire and water damage.

FARTHER/FURTHER

Farther is used when describing physical distance. *Further* means "more," as in to give more details.

We ran <u>farther</u> than I ever thought possible.

I asked the instructor to explain her lesson <u>further</u>.

THROUGH/THOROUGH/THOUGH/THRU

Through denotes traversing or passing beyond. *Thorough* means complete, rigorous, full. *Though* is another word for *but* or *excepting*. *Thru* should not be used.

We drove <u>through</u> the woods to reach grandmother's house.

Her work left no stone unturned, no idea unexamined; she proved herself a <u>thorough</u> and intelligent writer.

Accepting truth is a difficult, <u>though</u> necessary, part of life.

CITE/SITE/SIGHT

To *cite* means to note or give credit to (a source). A *site* is a physical location. *Sight* is a vision perceived through one's eyes.

Instructors require students to <u>cite</u> their sources when writing essays.

The attorney <u>cited</u> a prior court ruling to establish precedence.

The World Trade Center <u>site</u> in New York City is an incredibly sad but hopeful and inspiring place.

The <u>sight</u> of him brought tears to my eyes.

THAN/THEN

Than is used in a comparison. *Then* is an expression of a moment or a position in time.

My afternoon class is harder <u>than</u> my morning ones.

We went all over town, first to this store, <u>then</u> to that one.

ALL TOGETHER/ALTOGETHER

All together (two words) denotes people or things coming together in the same place. *Altogether* (one word) means "entirely, completely, in sum."

> We were <u>all together</u> for our last meal with him before he left to go to college.

> It was <u>altogether</u> ridiculous that we had to pay *and* wait in line.

SINCE/SENSE/CENTS/SCENTS

Since is another word for *because*. *Sense* is logic, reason, or intelligence. *Cents* are coins or money. *Scents* are aromas or smells.

> <u>Since</u> he did not have the <u>sense</u> to buy a nice-smelling candle with the few <u>cents</u> we had left to spend, we are stuck with these awful <u>scents</u> of mulberry and pinecone.

ASSURING PROPER USAGE

Study the correct usage of the following terms to help clarify and polish your work.

LESS/FEWER

Less is used to describe intangible, immeasurable quantities. *Fewer* is used to describe countable items.

> We have less <u>money</u> than we did before, which means <u>fewer</u> dollars to spend.

I/ME

To decide whether to use *I* or *me* in a sentence, follow the two rules listed below.

RULE 1: Finish the thought completely to see which pronoun would fit correctly in the sentence with the complete thought expressed.

> My brother is taller than <u>I/me</u>. (Finish the sentence: My brother is taller than <u>I am</u>. So, use *I*.)
>
> **CORRECT:** My brother is taller than <u>I</u>.

RULE 2: Look at the placement of the pronoun in question; if it follows a preposition (*about, above, across, with, to, for, by*, etc.), use *me*.

> He always buys the best presents for <u>I/me</u>. (The pronoun comes after a preposition, *for*, so we must use *me*.)
>
> **CORRECT:** He always buys the best presents for <u>me</u>.

RULE 3: In a compound sentence with two or more pronouns, drop the other pronouns to see whether *I* or *me* would be correct.

> They should let my group and <u>I/me</u> speak (You would not say, "Let *I* speak." (You would say, "Let *me* speak," so the proper pronoun here would be *me*.)
>
> **CORRECT:** They should let my group and <u>me</u> speak.

WHO/WHOM

To decide whether to use *who* or *whom*, replace the word in question with either *he* or *him*; if you can properly use the word *he*, then use *who*; if you can properly use *him*, then use *whom*. (Sometimes you may have to reorder the sentence, especially in interrogative sentences.)

He = who

Hi**m** = who**m** (Remember, both end with the letter *m*)

According to <u>who/whom</u>? (Rewrite the sentence to replace the "who/m" with either *he* or *him*. Which would be correct?: According to "he" or according to "him"? Since we would say according to "him," we would use *whom*, not *who*.)

CORRECT: According to <u>whom</u>?

THAT/WHICH

That introduces essential information to follow. *Which* introduces nonessential information to follow.

The book <u>that</u> I checked out from the library is now past due.

The proposed bill, <u>which</u> was written by Senator Cain, did not become ratified until the end of the session.

Remember this rule of thumb: When you introduce nonessential information with *which*, use a comma. When you introduce essential information with *that*, do not use a comma.

Which = comma

That = no comma

GOOD/WELL

Good is an adjective. *Well* is an adverb.

Use *good* to modify nouns:

the <u>good</u> book, <u>good</u> film, or <u>good</u> idea

Use *well* to modify verbs:

CORRECT: She writes <u>well</u>.

CORRECT: He sings <u>well.</u>

CORRECT: They play tennis <u>well</u>

Note the exception to this rule: We can correctly use either *good* or *well* to express states of being or health.

CORRECT: We feel <u>good</u> today.

CORRECT: I am <u>good</u>.

CORRECT: I feel <u>well</u> today.

CORRECT: I am <u>well</u>.

Remember, the exception *only* applies to states of being and health, not to actions.

INCORRECT: He hits the ball <u>good</u> for a beginner.

CORRECT: He hits the ball <u>well</u> for a beginner.

ON PRONOUNS

All three major academic style guides (the APA, MLA, and *The Chicago Manual of Style*) agree that a person's correct personal pronouns (they, he, she, ze, per, hir, etc.) should be respected and used in academic writing. In other words, regardless of your major, it's almost certain your professors expect you'll use correct personal pronouns when referring to others in your work. So, let's look at some quick tips and examples for pronoun usage to ensure we achieve this inclusivity and precision in our writing.

TIP #1: ASK OR LOOK UP THE PERSON'S PREFERRED PRONOUNS . . .

If the person about whom you are writing or speaking is a renowned scholar, writer, or otherwise well-known living human being, they likely have a website or social media page. Scour it to see which pronouns they prefer.

If you can simply ask the person about whom you're writing, then do so.

For example, try these questions:

- "May I ask what pronouns you prefer?"
- "How would you like me to refer to you in my work?"
- "How would you like to be addressed?"

TIP #2: PERHAPS YOU DON'T NEED A PRONOUN AT ALL . . .

When referencing an individual in your work, ask yourself if you could simply omit the pronoun.

EXAMPLE, WITH PRONOUN:

> When <u>he</u> spoke of the cultural significance of fairy tales, scholar Jack Zipes argued that in <u>his</u> opinion . . .

REVISED EXAMPLE, WITHOUT A PRONOUN:

> *Renowned fairy tale scholar Jack Zipes spoke convincingly of the cultural significance of fairy tales by arguing that . . .*

TIP #3: RECAST THE SUBJECT AS PLURAL INSTEAD OF SINGULAR AND USE "THEY" TO MINIMIZE EXCLUSION

EXAMPLE:

> *A student must use <u>her</u> time wisely and balance not only <u>her</u> school and personal life but also her work and romantic life, too.*

REVISED EXAMPLE:

> *Students must use <u>their</u> time wisely and balance not only <u>their</u> school and personal lives but also <u>their</u> work and romantic lives, too.*

TIP #4: USE "THEY" TO REFER TO A NON-SPECIFIC INDIVIDUAL OR TO AN INDIVIDUAL WHOSE PRONOUNS ARE UNKNOWN OR IRRELEVANT

EXAMPLE 1:

> **NO:** *Each contest entrant must turn in <u>his</u> entry by next Friday.*
> **WHY:** Unless the contest requires all entrants be male, we must edit our language to achieve greater inclusivity and accuracy here.
> **YES:** *Each contest entrant must turn in <u>their</u> entry by next Friday.*

EXAMPLE 2:

> **NO:** *A kind person goes out of her way for others, particularly when there's no personal gain for her.*
>
> **WHY:** If we use only the "feminine" pronoun "she," our reader may believe we're suggesting only females who use the pronouns she/hers can be kind.
>
> Clearly, this is not the case, so we must fix this issue.
>
> **YES:** *A kind person goes out of their way for others, particularly when there's no personal gain for them.*

Admittedly, it can be challenging to remember to pay close attention to the pronouns we use in our work and speech.

However, the solution here is this: Just keep *practicing*.

The more aware you become of *every word* used in your work, the more precise and defined your language will be. Your readers will certainly notice and appreciate it, and *you*, too, will appreciate it. All that attention to detail will mold you into a more skillful and powerful writer.

CAPITALIZATION

You are probably familiar with the basic rules of capitalization, such as capitalizing other people's names, the pronoun *I*, or the first word in a sentence. However, study the lesser-known rules to ensure you understand when to capitalize.

CAPITALIZE:

- Proper Nouns (names of specific people, places, and things)
  - Languages (English, French, Latin)
  - *Specific* course titles (*College Mathematics 1342*)
  - *Major* words (such as nouns, adjectives, and verbs) in titles of artistic works; do *not* capitalize prepositions, conjunctions, or articles, such as *of, and, the,* or *an*—unless they are the first word of the title (*The Sound and the Fury, The Lord of the Rings,* "What a Wonderful World," *Return of the Jedi*)
  - *Specific* place, region, or business titles (Mount Vesuvius, The Rocky Mountains, The South, New York Public Library, United American Bank)
  - Titles *when they precede the corresponding name* (Representative Hardwick, Doctor Dowdy, Aunt Debbie, Uncle Larry, Mayor Quimby)
  - Holidays, days of the week, months of the year (Christmas, Tuesday, September)
  - Countries, cities, and states (Belgium, San Francisco, Texas)
  - Street names, important buildings, and structures (Maple Street, The Empire State Building, The Washington Monument)
  - Major historic events and time periods (The Civil War, The Italian Renaissance, The English Enlightenment, World War II)

ESSENTIAL WRITING SKILLS FOR COLLEGE & BEYOND

- Names of *specific* deities and holy books (God, Zeus, Athena, Yahweh, Allah, the Bible, the Torah, the Bhagavad Gita)
- First Words
    - The first word in a direct quote, *if* the quote comprises a complete sentence

    Thoreau wrote, "If you have built castles in the air, your work need not be lost; that is where they should be. Now put the foundations under them."

    - The first word following a colon, *if* a complete sentence follows the colon

    Students must note the following announcement: Finals are cancelled.

DO NOT CAPITALIZE:

- Common Nouns
    - Seasons (spring, autumn, summer, winter)
    - Disciplines (history, mathematics, art, education)
    - General places or business types (library, museum, bank, mall)
    - Titles without corresponding names (representative, doctor, judge, aunt)
    - Directions (east, west, north, south)
    - General places or bodies of water (mountain, hill, ocean, river, lake)

EXAMPLES

Study the following capitalization examples to test your knowledge. If you want further practice, you can download the grammar, spelling, and punctuation test at www.writersdigest.com/essential-college-writing.

EXAMPLE 1

> **INCORRECT:** My University Math class is harder than I thought it would be.
>
> **CORRECT:** My university math class is harder than I thought it would be.

EXAMPLE 2

> **INCORRECT:** Our History Professor earned her degree from Harvard university.
>
> **CORRECT:** Our history professor earned her degree from Harvard University.

EXAMPLE 3

> **INCORRECT:** Mr. Jenkins, my Doctor, said I needed to take some Medication for my sore throat. He recommended something called allergin.
>
> **CORRECT:** Mr. Jenkins, my doctor, said I needed to take some medication for my sore throat. He recommended something called Allergin.

EXAMPLE 4

> **INCORRECT:** I went to the Library, but I turned West instead of North, so I ended up on Mary street.
>
> **CORRECT:** I went to the library, but I turned west instead of north, so I ended up on Mary Street.
>
> **CORRECT:** I went to the Manchaca Library, but I turned west instead of north, so I ended up on Mary Street.

EXAMPLE 5

> **INCORRECT:** This Fall, I hope to travel to europe sometime in October so I can go to Paris and visit the Eiffel

tower, see the great River running through the city, and brush up on my french.

CORRECT: This fall, I hope to travel to Europe sometime in October so I can go to Paris and visit the Eiffel Tower, see the great river running through the city, and brush up on my French.

EXAMPLE 6

INCORRECT: In my American history 1301 class, we are studying the civil war, and professor Rathbone told us this particular war was "The bloodiest in American History."

CORRECT: In my American History 1301 class, we are studying The Civil War, and Professor Rathbone told us this particular war was "the bloodiest in American history."

→ CHAPTER 9 →

Punctuation and Mechanics

Punctuation? Who cares?!

If you have ever asked this question, you are not alone. However, *you* should absolutely care about learning to use punctuation properly. Why? Punctuation helps you to communicate your ideas clearly and to ensure readers understand *exactly* what you mean to convey.

> *Correct, effective punctuation usage will increase the scores you earn on virtually all the writing assignments you turn in, regardless of the discipline.*

It helps to understand why we invented and use these marks we call "punctuation." Punctuation is a human invention designed for a specific purpose: meaning.

Punctuation allows writers to convey specific meanings. Just as we use voice tone and inflection in speech to convey emotions, imply sarcasm, or emphasize a point, so, too, do writers use punctuation to ensure their readers understand precisely what they mean.

For example, consider the striking difference between the following two sentences, which inspired a best-selling book on punctuation:

The panda bear eats, shoots, and leaves.
The panda bear eats shoots and leaves.

Do the sentences express the same meaning? They contain the exact same language and phrasing. Yet, they convey starkly different meanings. Which do you think the author *meant* to convey?

The mere addition of two tiny marks, the commas, dramatically changes the first sentence's meaning. The placement of commas marks the words "eats, shoots, and leaves" as a list of verbs, and thus the subject (the panda bear) is the agent who performs these actions. The sentence conveys the thought that the panda bear consumes food, fires a gun, and then departs the scene. The removal of the commas (as in the second sentence) fixes the problem and conveys the meaning that the writer most likely intended: The panda bear eats some plants, specifically "shoots and leaves." Clearly, punctuation can play an important role in constructing meaning. (If you find this discussion of punctuation interesting, check out Lynne Trusse's book *Eats, Shoots & Leaves*.)

Almost all communication in the digital age is written. Composing e-mails, texts, presentations, résumés, and memos requires knowledge of how to write well. Even socially, we are increasingly relying on writing to communicate: in e-mail, social networks, blogs, and web pages.

> *How well you present yourself in writing may dictate not only what grades you earn, but what jobs, contracts, and promotions you land.*

Knowing how to use punctuation means arming yourself to write anything for anyone at any time. Punctuation rules do not change; once you know them, you know them. A writer who does not know them, though, is much like a mechanic who cannot use a socket wrench or a painter who can paint with only a few types of brushes.

The good news is that learning the rules of punctuation is not difficult or painful and investing time in mastering the rules pays large dividends.

The benefits of learning punctuation rules include the following:

- **HIGHER SCORES.** Obviously a working knowledge of these rules will earn you higher scores. Instructors cannot and will not assign a high score to an essay that repeatedly misuses or omits punctuation marks.

- **INCREASED CONFIDENCE AND FREE TIME.** The fewer rules you have to look up and worry that you are misusing, the more time and energy you can devote to actually *writing*. Once you know the major punctuation rules, you can focus on conveying what you know instead of trying to figure out if that comma should or should not go here or there.
- **MORE SOPHISTICATED, POLISHED, AND IMPRESSIVE WORK.** Strong knowledge of punctuation can also help you vary your sentence structure, which means you will have the ability to create impressive, sophisticated sentences without fear of improperly punctuating them. This knowledge comes in handy anytime you need or want to write—whether for a class, a job, or a promotion.

Study the rules of punctuation outlined on the following pages, and practice until you master them. Feel free to skip around and learn whichever rules you feel most comfortable with first.

THE COMMA (,)

The comma is a mark of separation and pause. Use it to separate items (ideas, nouns, adjectives, verbs) in a sentence or to cause your reader to pause. Study the seven rules below to learn how to use the comma effectively, and remember this rule: *Only* insert a comma into a sentence when you can cite a rule to justify its inclusion—no rule, no comma.

RULE 1: Use a comma to separate three or more words, clauses, or phrases written in a series. Place a comma after each item except the last.[1]

> **INCORRECT:** The painting brilliantly used color composition and technique to inspire.
>
> **CORRECT:** The painting brilliantly used color, composition, and technique to inspire.
>
> **POSSIBLY INCORRECT:** The painting brilliantly used color, composition and technique to inspire. (Remember, scholars within different disciplines disagree on whether we must use a comma before the final item, so check with your professor.)

Since this rule is so widely known, many people often forget its importance, but it is easily remembered by the earlier referenced example from *Eats, Shoots & Leaves*. Remember, this rule applies not only to noun series, but also to verbs, adjectives, and even clauses if presented in a series of three or more.

> **CORRECT:** She twists, turns, and jumps all over the mat.
>
> **CORRECT:** The dilapidated, rusting, ancient home remains for sale.

---

[1] In some disciplines, such as journalism, placing the comma before the final item in the list is optional; however, the *MLA Handbook* advocates for its inclusion, so if you are uncertain what your professor prefers, just ask.

CORRECT: She decided to move away from home, join the Peace Corps, and volunteer in Guam.

RULE 2: Use a comma to separate coordinate adjectives. Coordinate adjectives work together to describe or modify a noun; coordinate adjectives are not connected by *and*.

INCORRECT: Faulkner is a brilliant beautiful writer.
INCORRECT: Faulkner is a brilliant, and beautiful writer.
CORRECT: Faulkner is a brilliant, beautiful writer.

Do not use a comma to separate noncoordinate adjectives. Coordinate adjectives separately modify the noun.

EXAMPLE: The <u>frayed, bulky</u> sweater was surprisingly expensive.

Both *frayed* and *bulky* each describe the sweater. They do not build on each other or rely on each other for their meaning, but they do work together to create a picture for us of the sweater. We know it is both frayed and bulky.

Noncoordinate adjectives do not separately modify the noun. Instead, they build on each other. The first adjective modifies the second adjective, which then modifies the noun.

EXAMPLE: She wrote her book about her childhood home, a <u>yellow frame</u> house.

Yellow describes the color of the frame, not necessarily the house, so we would not want to separate *yellow* from *frame* with a comma.

INCORRECT: The bright, red car glistened in the sun.
CORRECT: The bright red car glistened in the sun.

The word *bright* modifies *red*, not *car* (What kind of red was the car? It was *bright* red. It was not the car that was bright but the red paint), so we do not need to separate the adjectives with a comma because they are noncoordinate adjectives.

RULE 3: Use a comma to set off appositives. Appositives are nonessential information in a sentence; in other words, an appositive gives readers additional information that is *not* crucial to the sentence's meaning. An appositive is like an aside, something said in passing, or bonus information.

> **INCORRECT:** My professor, Dr. Cohen is a brilliant scholar and grammarian.
>
> **CORRECT:** My professor, Dr. Cohen, is a brilliant scholar and grammarian.

In the second sentence, the writer has correctly marked the professor's name, Dr. Cohen, as an appositive. By setting it off with commas, the writer tells us this information is not crucial to the meaning of the sentence. The sentence would still make sense and retain its essential meaning: "My professor is a brilliant scholar and grammarian." We may not know the professor's name, but we would still understand the core meaning.

> **INCORRECT:** The chief of police an expert in police procedure wrote an interesting, insightful book on life as an officer of the law.
>
> **CORRECT:** The chief of police, an expert in police procedure, wrote an interesting, insightful book on life as an officer of the law.

The appositive information, "an expert in police procedure," must be set off by commas because it is additional information and leaving it in creates a run-on sentence, which is confusing to understand.

> **INCORRECT:** Students, who cheat, will fail.
>
> **CORRECT:** Students who cheat will fail.

In this case, the writer should *not* mark "who cheat" as an appositive. This information is crucial to the meaning of the sentence. If we remove it, we drastically alter the sentence's message: "Students will fail" conveys an entirely different meaning than "Students who cheat will fail."

The writer should remove the commas to fix this error so that the sentence reads: "Students who cheat will fail."

RULE 4: Place a comma after introductory clauses and phrases four words or longer or after one-word introductions. Introductory words, phrases, and clauses work to set the stage for the main idea or action of the sentence. They offer readers introductory information but do *not* contain the subject or verb of the sentence.

SAMPLE INTRODUCTORY WORDS AND PHRASES

- However,
- On the other hand,
- Also,
- When I was a kid,
- Thus,
- Once upon a time,
- Otherwise,
- In spite of recent evidence,
- Rather,
- For example,
- Yet,
- Indeed,
- Because of his desire to win,
- Hence,
- After a long-winded debate,

INCORRECT: The ruling was unexpected. However it was fair.

CORRECT: The ruling was unexpected. However, it was fair.

INCORRECT: When I was a child in Africa I spent most of my time searching for food and shelter.

CORRECT: When I was a child in Africa, I spent most of my time searching for food and shelter.

INCORRECT: Learning the business, was one of the most difficult things he ever attempted.

CORRECT: Learning the business was one of the most difficult things he ever attempted.

In Example 3, the writer should *not* place a comma after *business* because "learning the business" works as the sentence's subject, not as an introduction to the main action of the sentence.

RULE 5: Place a comma after each of the following: the names of cities, states, dates, and years.

INCORRECT: Valentine's Day is February 14 2014 a Friday.

CORRECT: Valentine's Day is February 14, 2014, a Friday.

INCORRECT: San Antonio Texas is the hometown of writer Sandra Cisneros.

CORRECT: San Antonio, Texas, is the hometown of writer Sandra Cisneros.

RULE 6: Use a comma to join two independent clauses connected by a coordinating conjunction. Be sure you have *two independent* clauses, not one independent clause and one dependent clause. An independent clause is a clause (a group of words) that can stand alone, meaning it does not need any other portion of the sentence to make sense. It has a subject and a verb, and it presents a complete thought. A dependent clause is a clause that cannot stand alone. A coordinating conjunction connects ideas. Remember them by using the acronym FANBOYS:

> For
> And
> Nor
> But
> Or
> Yet
> So

Ensure that you include a FANBOY when you connect two independent clauses with a comma. Otherwise, the sentence will not be punctuated correctly.

> **INCORRECT:** I want to go to Europe this summer with my friends but I don't have the money.
>
> **CORRECT:** I want to go to Europe this summer with my friends, but I don't have the money.

The first clause, "I want to go to Europe this summer," is independent; it has a subject (*I*) and a verb (*want*). It also presents a complete thought. We could place a period after *summer* because this clause is strong enough to form its own sentence. The second clause, "I don't have the money," is also an independent clause. These two independent clauses are joined by a coordinating conjunction (*but*), and thus we place a comma before the conjunction to adhere to the rule.

> **INCORRECT:** Thomas went to the store, and bought two loaves of bread.
>
> **CORRECT:** Thomas went to the store and bought two loaves of bread.
>
> **CORRECT:** Thomas went to the store, and he bought two loaves of bread.

The first clause, "Thomas went to the store," is independent, but what about the second clause ("bought two loaves of bread")? Remember, an independent clause must be able to stand alone—it must have its own subject and verb and express a complete thought. Is "bought two loaves of bread" a complete thought? Who bought these items? We must look to the other clause ("Thomas went to the store") to find out it was Thomas, which means the clause "bought two loaves of bread" is dependent on the first clause for its meaning. Thus, this sentence does not adhere to the rule, and we should either delete the comma or add a subject, such as *he*.

> **INCORRECT:** She is the best friend I've ever had, I love her.

The writer has incorrectly punctuated this sentence because it contains two independent clauses joined by a comma *without* a coordinating conjunction (FANBOY). The writer can fix this sentence with either of these strategies:

1. Adding a FANBOY after the comma

   CORRECT: She is the best friend I've ever had, <u>and</u> I love her.

2. Changing the comma to a semicolon

   CORRECT: She is the best friend I've ever had; I love her.

RULE 7: Use the comma to introduce a quotation following a dependent clause (use the colon to set up a quotation following an independent clause).

   INCORRECT: According to Thoreau "The mass of men lead lives of quiet desperation" (50).
   INCORRECT: According to Thoreau: "The mass of men lead lives of quiet desperation" (50).
   CORRECT: According to Thoreau, "The mass of men lead lives of quiet desperation" (50).

Do *not* use the comma to introduce the quote if you incorporate the quote into the flow of your own phrasing.

   INCORRECT: According to Thoreau, most people, "lead lives of quiet desperation" (50).
   CORRECT: According to Thoreau, most people "lead lives of quiet desperation" (50).

THE SEMICOLON (;)

The semicolon, like the comma, is among the most misused punctuation marks in the English language. Study the two semicolon placement rules to create longer, more sophisticated sentences; the semicolon can also help you connect ideas within a single sentence and thus vary your sentence structure.

RULE 1: Use the semicolon to join two independent clauses. As mentioned in the section on commas, an independent clause is a clause that can stand alone. It could form its own sentence (it has both a subject and a verb, and it expresses a complete thought).

> **INCORRECT:** I have learned a great deal in my writing class, now I know I am a strong writer.
> **CORRECT:** I have learned a great deal in my writing class; now I know I am a strong writer.
> **CORRECT:** I have learned a great deal in my writing class. Now I know I am a strong writer.

The first sentence of the above example is incorrect because there is not a coordinating conjunction (one of the FANBOYS) to connect the two independent clauses. The writer needs to either (1) add a coordinating conjunction or (2) change the comma to a semicolon. The second sentence in the example is correctly punctuated because it joins two independent clauses; each clause contains a subject and a verb and could stand on its own as a full sentence.

You may wonder why the writer would choose a semicolon rather than, say, a period. Consider the difference, as presented in the third sentence. The writer has correctly punctuated both sentences. Whether the writer chooses to use a semicolon or a period is simply a matter of stylistic choice. The writer uses the period to create two distinct sentences to stress the ideas in both by placing them within their own sentences. However, be sure this emphasis is warranted. Writing an essay that includes all simple sentences (meaning no complex, sophisticated sentences) will make for stilted, choppy writing.

RULE 2: Use the semicolon to separate items in a series in which the items themselves contain commas.

> **INCORRECT:** We expect the following people to attend today's luncheon: Nancy Wilson, Writing Center Director, Nadine Cooper, Director of Undergraduate Studies, and Susan Beebe, Dean of Student Services.
>
> **CORRECT:** We expect the following people to attend today's luncheon: Nancy Wilson, Writing Center Director; Nadine Cooper, Director of Undergraduate Studies; and Susan Beebe, Dean of Student Services.

In the first list, the names and titles of the attendees are indistinguishable. Who is the Writing Center Director? Is it Nancy Wilson or Nadine Cooper? Perhaps the director is yet another person who remains unnamed? By listing these names and titles with commas, the writer unfortunately makes the information unnecessarily confusing. By replacing the commas after the titles, the writer can easily distinguish which title belongs with which person.

You probably noticed that one of the semicolon rules is very similar to the comma rule, and in fact students usually interpose the two marks. To avoid this problem, download the exercise at www.writers digest.com/essential-college-writing.

THE COLON (:)

Many students shy away from using the colon; they know it's a punctuation mark, but they are uncertain of its rules and have trouble distinguishing it from the semicolon. The colon, however, is an important punctuation mark and a powerful tool for conveying meaning. It looks like two periods stacked on top of each other, whereas a semicolon is a period on top of a comma.

The two punctuation marks have different rules for their usage, but fear not; these rules are easy to learn, and they're worth the effort. The colon is especially handy for two purposes: (1) introducing lists and (2) leading a reader to a conclusion or point you wish to highlight.

RULE 1: Use the colon to introduce a list; be sure the clause preceding the colon is independent. (Look to the left of the colon; the clause to the *left* of the colon must be independent.)

> **INCORRECT:** Friends to invite: Jonathan, Patricia, Chris, Julie, Tanya, Karmen, Lynda, Nicole, Paul, and Tiffani.
>
> **CORRECT:** She has many friends to invite: Jonathan, Patricia, Chris, Julie, Tanya, Karmen, Lynda, Nicole, Paul, and Tiffani.

RULE 2: Use a colon after an independent clause to introduce and highlight a quotation.

> **INCORRECT:** Emerson: "To be yourself in a world that is constantly trying to make you something else is the greatest accomplishment."
>
> **CORRECT:** Emerson's view on identity is perhaps the most succinct of the three writers: "To be yourself in a world that is constantly trying to make you something else is the greatest accomplishment."

RULE 3: Use a colon in complex sentences to lead readers to a conclusion or to highlight a point—be sure the clause to the *left* of the colon is independent.

> **INCORRECT:** Colbert's character: He is a satirical spoof meant to expose and criticize societal cruelty and injustice.
>
> **CORRECT:** Viewers appalled by the supposed cruelty of TV's Stephen Colbert of *The Colbert Report* miss the overall point: The character Colbert plays is a satirical spoof meant to expose and criticize societal cruelty and injustice.

RULE 4: Place a colon after the salutation of a professional or business letter.

> **INCORRECT:** Dear Professor Smith,
> **CORRECT:** Dear Professor Smith:

Most instructors agree that using a comma for a personal letter or e-mail is acceptable; however, when writing business letters and other professional correspondences, place a colon after the salutation.

RULE 5: Use a colon to separate hours and minutes in expressions of time.

> **INCORRECT:** She set the appointment for 1130 a.m.
> **CORRECT:** She set the appointment for 11:30 a.m.

ITALICS

RULE 1: Use italics to stress words or phrases. Use this strategy sparingly, as overusing it will nullify its effect and in many cases will confuse readers.

> **INCORRECT:** Viewers must *note* that it is *Mildred* who takes the *blame* for the *murder, not* Bert.
>
> **CORRECT:** Viewers must note that it is *Mildred* who takes the blame for the murder, not Bert.

RULE 2: Italicize (do not underline) the titles of larger works, such as books, films, epic poems, reference works, journals, magazines, newspapers, websites, and television shows.[2]

> **INCORRECT:** The television program <u>Family Guy</u> reveals a great deal about competing notions of masculinity within American culture.
>
> **CORRECT:** The television program *Family Guy* reveals a great deal about competing notions of masculinity within American culture.
>
> **INCORRECT:** Growing up, I read Mark Twain's "The Adventures of Huckleberry Finn" religiously.
>
> **CORRECT:** Growing up, I read Mark Twain's *The Adventures of Huckleberry Finn* religiously.

RULE 3: Use italics to introduce terms or words from another language.

> **INCORRECT:** The term fiancé has French origins.
>
> **CORRECT:** The term *fiancé* has French origins.

---

[2] The 2009 edition of the *MLA Handbook*, the authority on punctuation use in North America, officially banned the use of underlining for titles of major works. Though you may have learned in previous classes that the writer can either underline or italicize the titles of large works so long as this use remained consistent throughout the work, now writers *must* italicize, not underline.

DASHES, HYPHENS, AND PARENTHESES

THE DASH (—)

Use the dash to emphasize key phrases and information and to highlight important elements of your paper for readers. (You can type a dash into your document by hitting the hyphen key twice.)

RULE: Always use dashes in pairs, unless the information you wish to highlight appears at the end of the sentence.

> **INCORRECT:** Presumed—not confirmed dead, Elvis Presley is my favorite artist of all time.
> **CORRECT:** Presumed—not confirmed—dead, Elvis Presley is my favorite artist of all time.

The writer should enclose the words "not confirmed" within the dashes to highlight their importance. Otherwise, the sentence loses its flow and clarity—and it would be punctuated incorrectly. Dashes work like arrows to point to the importance of certain information within a sentence, thereby indicating stress. In fact, the dash is the highest form of stress a writer can use with punctuation (parentheses are second highest, and commas are the lowest).

> **INCORRECT:** William Faulkner's work and life are fascinating—and he is among the most important writers—of the twentieth century.
> **CORRECT:** William Faulkner's work and life are fascinating—and he is among the most important writers of the twentieth century.

In this example, the writer need not include another dash in the sentence; all the words following the dash work to express what information the writer wishes to highlight—that he believes Faulkner to be among the most important writers of the twentieth century.

THE HYPHEN (-)

RULE 1: Use the hyphen to spell out numbers twenty-one through ninety-nine.

> **INCORRECT:** Twenty three people attended our party last night.
>
> **CORRECT:** Twenty-three people attended our party last night.

RULE 2: Use the hyphen for compound adjectives (two or more adjectives used as a unit to modify a noun).

> **INCORRECT:** Last semester, I took a twentieth century philosophy class.
>
> **CORRECT:** Last semester, I took a twentieth-century philosophy class.

The two words *twentieth* and *century* work as a unit to modify the noun *philosophy*, so we must hyphenate them.

Do *not* use a hyphen with one-word adjectives or with an adjective/adverb modifier.

> **INCORRECT:** My class examines American history of the twentieth-century.
>
> **CORRECT:** My class examines American history of the twentieth century.
>
> **INCORRECT:** He wrote a poorly-constructed outline of his essay.
>
> **CORRECT:** He wrote a poorly constructed outline of his essay.

PARENTHESES ( )

RULE 1: Use parentheses to enclose additional, nonessential information (an aside or a clarification). Ensure the information within parentheses is truly extra and not crucial to the reader's understanding of the sentence's meaning.

INCORRECT: (My sister) who lives in Tennessee gave birth last week.

CORRECT: My sister (who lives in Tennessee) gave birth last week.

RULE 2: Periods go *inside* parentheses only if an entire sentence is inside the parentheses.

INCORRECT: Please read the report (enclosed as Attachment 1.)

CORRECT: Please read the report (enclosed as Attachment 1).

CORRECT: Please be sure to read the report. (You will find it under "Reports" on the Employment link on our web page.)

QUOTATION MARKS ("")

We use quotation marks primarily to do exactly what their name implies: to mark quotations. However, they do serve a few other useful purposes, such as serving as a place marker for omitted letters and numbers. Note in particular the distinctions listed below in using quotation marks properly, including when to use double ("") versus single (') quotation marks.

RULE 1: Place *double* quotation marks around a direct quotation, meaning a statement taken directly from a speech or text.

> **INCORRECT:** Mahatma Ghandi's famous statement, Be the change you wish to see in the world, clearly had a profound impact on Martin's work.
>
> **CORRECT:** Mahatma Ghandi's famous statement, "Be the change you wish to see in the world," clearly had a profound impact on Martin's work.

RULE 2: Place *double* quotation marks around the titles of smaller works, such as short stories, essays, newspaper articles, magazine articles, journal articles, song titles, most poems' titles, television episode titles, and chapter titles.

> **INCORRECT:** William Faulkner's short story *A Rose for Emily* remains a classic within American literature.
>
> **CORRECT:** William Faulkner's short story "A Rose for Emily" remains a classic within American literature.
>
> **INCORRECT:** *The Simpsons* episode Homer's Head addresses the deep-seated nature of American anti-intellectualism.
>
> **CORRECT:** *The Simpsons* episode "Homer's Head" addresses the deep-seated nature of American anti-intellectualism.

RULE 3: Use *double* quotation marks to cast suspicion on the meaning or usage of a term or phrase. For example, consider the differing meanings of the pairs of sentences below:

EXAMPLE 1:

The progress in Austin, TX, marches forward.
The "progress" in Austin, TX, marches forward.

EXAMPLE 2:

Real men wear pink.
"Real" men wear pink.

EXAMPLE 3:

The senator's concern for students' welfare was evident.
The senator's concern for "student welfare" was evident.

The pairs of sentences in all three examples contain the exact same phrasing, but do they relay the same meaning? The addition of the quotation marks alerts readers that the words within are to be understood ironically—and thus the meanings of the sentences drastically change with the addition of the quotation marks.

This strategy can be used to:

1. **CONVEY MEANING SUCCINCTLY.** Instead of simply writing out, "Other people praise the growth and urban development of Austin as 'progress,' but I don't believe it is," the writer of example 1 has quickly conveyed this message to readers by adding the quotation marks.

2. **DRAW ATTENTION TO CERTAIN WORDS AND/OR PHRASES.** The writer of example 2 draws our attention to the notion of "real" men by placing quotation marks around the word. This strategy allows the writer to confront the term and thus spur readers to think on it more deeply. For example, the writer may want readers to wonder: "What is a 'real' man? What does that term mean? Are there 'fake' men?"

Remember, encouraging readers to think more deeply on the topic is one of your goals as an academic writer. Using quotation marks to cast suspicion on terms or phrases can help you achieve this goal. However, be careful not to overuse this quotation mark function. If every other sentence you write contains an ironic use of quotation marks, they will lose their effect—and readers will become bored and irritated. Use them once, or twice at the most, in a five- to seven-page essay.

RULE 4: Use single quotations (') to mark a quotation within a quotation.

> **INCORRECT:** The reporter told us, "When I interviewed the winner and asked him about great writing, he simply said, "There is no secret. Only hard work, determination, and confidence."
>
> **CORRECT:** The reporter told us, "When I interviewed the winner and asked him about great writing, he simply said, 'There is no secret. Only hard work, determination, and confidence.'"

THE APOSTROPHE (')

The apostrophe has two primary uses: It represents omitted letters or numbers, and it shows possession.

RULE 1: Place the apostrophe in the position of the omitted letter(s) or number(s).

> **INCORRECT:** We dont have all the answers.
> **CORRECT:** We don't have all the answers.

The apostrophe represents the missing letter *o* from the word *not*. Thus we must place an apostrophe to stand in for the missing letter: "We do n<u>o</u>t have all the answers."

> **INCORRECT:** Many scholars write about the turbulence within the twentieth century, especially within the 60's.
> **CORRECT:** Many scholars write about the turbulence within the twentieth century, especially within the '60s.

The apostrophe represents the missing numbers 1 and 9 to indicate the century to which the writer refers, so we must place it where the omitted numbers would be: "Many scholars write about the turbulence within the twentieth century, especially within the <u>19</u>60s."

Exercise caution when using apostrophes to abbreviate decades; be sure you clearly establish what specific time period your work examines before using abbreviations to indicate a decade. For example, if you examine comedic family television texts of the 1960s, then it may be fine to write "in the '60s … ." However, when writers simply include a reference to the '40s, readers may not know whether the referenced decade is the 1940s, 1840s, 1740s, and so on. When in doubt, ask your instructor whether it is acceptable for you to use the apostrophe to abbreviate a decade. If you are uncertain, the safest bet is to include the century.

RULE 2: Use the apostrophe to indicate possession.

- **SINGULAR NOUNS:** Add an apostrophe and the letter *s* to the end of any singular noun to indicate possession.

    INCORRECT: The dogs bone sat on his dish.
    CORRECT: The dog's bone sat on his dish.

    This rule includes singular nouns that end in *s*.

    INCORRECT: Texas' laws on theft are harsher than virtually any other state's.
    CORRECT: Texas's laws on theft are harsher than virtually any other state's.[3]

- **PLURAL NOUNS:** Add only an apostrophe after the letter *s* of plural nouns to indicate possession. Do not add another *s*. Use *s'* only for words that are *both* plural and possessive.

    INCORRECT: The boys's books sit stacked on the desk.
    CORRECT: The boys' books sit stacked on the desk.

    Consider the difference between the following two sentences:

    The boy's books sit stacked on the desk.
    The boys' books sit stacked on the desk.

    The first sentence indicates that *one* boy's books sit stacked on a desk; the second sentence indicates that *multiple boys* have books that sit stacked on a desk.

---

[3] The second sentence often looks incorrect to many readers, and in fact different collegiate handbooks often offer conflicting information on this rule. So which method is correct and according to whom?

The writers of the 2021 edition of the *MLA Handbook* advocate the second example (add an apostrophe and an *s* to any singular noun to indicate possession—even those singular nouns ending in *s* [2.50 & 2.51, p. 33]). Since most academics turn first to this book with regard to grammar rules, I recommend you follow the advice of its authors. However, when in doubt, ask your instructor.

ELLIPSIS (...)

The ellipsis is a highly valuable, yet underutilized, punctuation mark because many students either do not know what it is, or they lack the confidence to use it. However, the ellipsis comes in handy, particularly when citing research, so it is to your benefit to learn how to use it properly.

The ellipsis is a set of three periods that indicate the omission of a word or set of words omitted from the citation of a quotation: (...)

Use the ellipsis to omit a word, phrase, or sentence from a source. You will likely encounter material that you wish to quote in your work, but you may not want to quote *all* of it. The ellipsis allows writers to use only the material needed from a source.

However, use caution when incorporating ellipses: Always heed the excellent advice contained within the *MLA Handbook* in relation to the use of ellipses. When including an ellipsis in your work, "be guided by two principles: fairness to the author quoted and the grammatical integrity of your writing. A quotation should never be presented in a way that could cause a reader to misunderstand the sense or meaning of the source" (272).

Follow the ellipses rules below to ensure proper usage.

RULE 1: For an ellipsis *within* a sentence, use three periods with a space before each and a space after the last:

ORIGINAL MATERIAL

"When we are unhurried and wise, we perceive that only great and worthy things have any permanent and absolute existence, that petty fears and petty pleasures are but the shadow of the reality" (Thoreau 139-40).

QUOTATION WITH ELLIPSIS

Thoreau encourages us to be more present and fight the urge to rush from one activity to the next. He teaches us that by slowing down, we can truly learn what is valuable:

> "When we are unhurried and wise . . . only great and wor-
> thy things have any permanent and absolute existence,
> that petty fears and petty pleasures are but the shadow
> of the reality" (Thoreau 139-40).

RULE 2: To use an ellipsis at the end of a sentence *followed by a cita-tion,* use three periods with a space before each and then place the sen-tence's period *after* the parenthesis. Do *not* place parentheses or brack-ets around ellipses—unless including them would clarify your use of the ellipses.

QUOTATION WITH ELLIPSIS

> Thoreau succinctly teaches us the value of taking our time:
> "When we are unhurried and wise, we perceive that only
> great and worthy things have any permanent and abso-
> lute existence . . ." (139-40).

PART IV
MAKING THE
GRADE

➻ CHAPTER 10 ➻

The Psychology of
Grading and Scoring

Will your paper earn an *A*, *B*, *C*, *D*, or *F*?

The classic grading spectrum is familiar to most American students, and not surprisingly, most students' assignments fall somewhere in the middle (*B*, *C*, or *D*). However, did you know instructors or graders can usually spot an *A* essay before they even read it? They can also typically spot an *F* essay just as easily.

This chapter will provide examples to help you see the distinct difference between student work that stands out as exceptional and professional and student work that unfortunately stands out as lazy, sloppy, and subpar.

As class sizes grow increasingly larger at both universities and community colleges, instructors know fewer and fewer of their students. This means your instructors will largely know you through your writing and not through personal interaction with you.

Therefore, the impression you make in writing will largely determine your instructor's perception of you as a student, meaning their perceptions of your abilities, intelligence, and potential as a scholar. In other words, your writing abilities will largely determine your final grade in many of your courses. If you want to earn the highest scores possible, you must learn to create a positive impression of yourself through your writing.

STRATEGIES TO IMPRESS YOUR GRADER

Use the following strategies to immediately impress your instructors. Many of these will seem intuitive, but you would be surprised how many papers I have graded (hundreds at least) that have earned failing grades simply for violating the following rules. Granted, your essay will not likely fail simply because you did not follow one of the rules listed below, but, depending on the instructor, violation of several of these rules in concert with other violations (such as grammar or logical errors) may add up to a failing score. Conversely, following these rules may earn you points that add up to a higher grade than you expected.

- Turn in assignments on time and in the way dictated by the assignment (whether digitally or on paper, in a folder or not, with rough draft or not, etc.).
- Contextualize *your discussion within a larger one:* Show the relation of *your* ideas to other scholars' arguments and theories. (The book *They Say, I Say* provides excellent resources that teach students how to perform this task well—see the list of suggested further reading in Appendix A for more information.)
- Cite plenty of evidence to support your claim(s).
- Give your work an interesting, pertinent title (*not* "Essay #4").
- Use your computer's spell-check function, and *double-check its work*; the spell-check feature is by no means perfect, so always ensure the accuracy of the spelling (including and especially your instructor's name, course title, and the titles and names of works and characters or people referenced in the essay).
- Proofread and edit your work, both on the computer and on paper—sometimes you may miss a mistake on the screen that you would not miss on the printed page.

- Go above and beyond the call of the assignment by offering in-depth research and specialized knowledge on the topic or text—but be careful not to ramble.
- Show up for peer review days.
- Ask your instructor if she will read your rough draft and give you feedback.
- Follow formatting instructions (headings, font sizes, cover pages, etc.).
- Heed the word count (do not turn in twelve pages for an eight-page assignment).
- Use black ink (no colored ink).
- Reprint if the ink is faded or difficult to read.

STRATEGIES TO ALIENATE, FRUSTRATE, AND ANNOY YOUR GRADER

If your goal is to ensure your essay will not pass and to make your work seem lazy and sloppy (and I hope that is *not* your goal), try the following strategies.

- **IGNORE THE PROMPT.** This point seems obvious, but it can be easy to get off track. Be sure your paper not only addresses the topic but also *answers the question posed by the prompt.* For example, if the essay asks students to discuss the importance of gender in contemporary film but the student instead discusses why *The Dark Knight Rises* is such a great and important film, that would be a quick road to an *F*. Beware of engaging in a rant on what *you* want to write about rather than what the assignment dictated. It's frustrating to write on a topic you find uninteresting, but not every prompt you receive in college will excite you. Write about it anyway, and try to *make* it interesting.

- **TURN IN CARELESS, SLOPPY WORK.** Typographical errors happen, and most instructors will forgive a few minor issues, especially in a long paper. However, an essay filled with typos smacks of sloppiness rather than honest mistakes.

- **ADD LOTS OF BLANK FILLER SPACE.** Beginning students often worry they did not write enough, so they use larger fonts or add many extra spaces in an attempt to make the essay seem longer. Doing so will fool no one (instructors were once students, too, and they already know this trick). It actually achieves the reverse effect by drawing attention to the blank spaces.

- **DON'T BOTHER TO CHECK FACTS.** When student writers do not check facts, such as character names, places, dates, and/or other important information, or if this information is misspelled, instructors worry about the student's ability to do well beyond the classroom. Conscientiousness is a highly regarded quality by instructors and employers alike, so beware of errors—for they will quickly spell disaster for the essay's grade.

- **ILLUSTRATE INADEQUATE KNOWLEDGE.** One of the quickest ways to alienate an instructor is to illustrate that you have little or no knowledge of the texts or concepts studied in class. Students who do not demonstrate that they paid attention during class and completed the necessary reading and analysis of the material receive low scores on their work.
- **IGNORE THE TYPE OF WRITING REQUIRED FOR THE ASSIGNMENT.** This error remains among the most common for beginning writers, so ensure your work does not merely summarize a text if the assignment calls for analysis or evaluation (few academic assignments will require *only* summarization).

EXCERPT

Visually compare the following examples of student work—don't read them yet, but visually scan each and try to develop an idea of the students and their abilities simply by impression.

STUDENT 1

Susan Q. Student

Professor V. Smith

English 1310

March 22, 2014

Ophelia's Beautiful Mess: Revealing the Life in Her Death

Shakespeare's *Hamlet* is among the most well-known documents of humanity. As a play, it is considered superb, and as a testament to human character, critics and readers alike hail it as a brilliant masterpiece. This is disturbing information, though, when considering the suicide of one of its only female characters: young, beautiful, tragic, Ophelia. Her suicide haunts readers, and even today, more than four hundred years later, readers continue to ask why. Many scholars argue that Ophelia either accidentally drowns or kills herself out of grief over losing her romantic connection with Hamlet. However, it is clear that Ophelia purposefully commits suicide, which illustrates to readers her lack of freedom and the realization of a crucial aspect of the rottenness in Denmark: Ophelia, as a female, could never truly be free.

STUDENT 2

Rita B. Student

Essay 4

No body knows for sure what Shakespeare meant by this play, esp. about Ophelia. Lots of people wonder why Ophelia did what she did.

That's why so many scholars have written so much about it and have tried to figure it out. And that's what my paper is going to talk about too.

Ophelia was young and innocent. She had a relationship with Hamlet, but he was mad at her and told her to become a nun.

Which paper looks more professional? Which student invested more time and energy in the assignment? The following highlights differences in the students' work.

STUDENT 1

- Uses the standard 12-point, Times New Roman font
- Includes a heading with pertinent course information
- Gives the essay an original, interesting title
- Uses conventional spacing

STUDENT 2

- Uses a larger font to attempt to make her work look more substantial than it is (This "trick" is probably the oldest one in the book; it will *not* work!)
- Includes no heading
- Titles the paper "Essay 4" instead of giving it a more compelling and relevant title

Clearly, the first student distinguishes herself as a polished and professional student writer. Unfortunately, the second student's essay looks unprofessional and thrown together, and the lack of information and depth of thought will mean disaster for the grade.

Is it unfair of an instructor to judge the entire paper simply by how it *appears*? *Unfair* is a subjective term, and most instructors would say no. Think of it this way: Would a job applicant who turned in a sloppy application get the job—or even an interview? Would a scholarship applicant with a similarly unpolished application beat out the competition? Not likely. Besides, instructors know from experience that failure to attend to detail at the beginning of the essay rarely transforms later into smart, in-depth analysis as the essay continues.

Now go back and read the examples to see whether the formatting and spacing issues do indeed prove indicative of the content. You'll see that the first student's work is not perfect, but it clearly demonstrates the student's thinking on the play and her opinion of Ophelia's importance within it. The second student's work, however, does not present any clear perspective on the play. It simply summarizes it and mentions the questions *others* raise without presenting any answers to or perspectives on these questions.

PLACE YOURSELF IN THE INSTRUCTOR'S POSITION

If *you* were these students' instructor, would you feel comfortable passing Student 2's paper (assuming the quality of the introduction is representative of the paper's quality as a whole)? Would you feel confident sending this student on to more difficult courses, though she has not yet demonstrated the writing and analytical skills necessary to succeed? Passing this level of work would be unfair to this student, for it tells her that her current skill level will prepare her for the challenges she will face in future courses, and based on this work, that is unfortunately not true.

PLAGIARISM

What is the quickest, easiest way to fail an essay? Plagiarize it.

What is plagiarism? In a word, fraud. Remember the executives from Enron who were caught taking others' money and using it as though it was theirs all along? The academic equivalent of this offense is plagiarizing: taking someone else's words or ideas and passing them off as your own.

WHAT COUNTS AS PLAGIARISM?

- Cutting and pasting information from the Internet without citing the source
- Taking a passage, sentence, or even just an idea from any source (a web page, book, essay, article, etc.) without citing the source
- Rephrasing someone else's words without citing the source
- Buying a paper from an online essay-writing service
- Using a friend, roommate, or anyone else's paper as your own

The key to all of these examples is in the citation (giving credit to the source). U.S. law protects our written words and thoughts with copyright laws, and theft of these ideas and words is not only immoral but also illegal.

Penalties for this offense are severe. In addition to the fear of getting caught, plagiarizers risk a failing score on the assignment and in the entire course, expulsion from the college or university, and in some severe cases, criminal charges.

Fear not, though! Plagiarism is easy to avoid: Simply cite the source from which you first read or saw the ideas, words, or sentences you include in your work.

If you do not know how to cite the source properly, ask your instructor or reference librarian, visit your university writing center, or check online for citation guide websites (most universities have their own pages and sites on citation guides to help students). I recommend the following sites for easy reference:

- http://owl.english.purdue.edu/owl/section/2/
- http://www.library.cornell.edu/resrch/citmanage
- http://library.duke.edu/research/citing/

If you fear you cannot cite the source 100 percent perfectly, don't let that stop you from citing—ask for help, and then do the best you can. Even if the final citation is not perfect, it's better to cite incorrectly than to omit the citation entirely. An incorrect citation may cost you a few points, but not citing at all may cost you the entire course.

GRADING RUBRICS

A grading rubric is essentially a standardized scoring sheet instructors use to evaluate student assignments. Typically, rubrics outline the performance expected in different categories. For example, writing instructors may include the following categories.

- Thesis statement
- Introduction paragraph
- Body paragraphs
- Overall organization
- Grammar, spelling, and punctuation
- Proper citation of sources

USE THE RUBRIC TO YOUR ADVANTAGE

BEFORE TURNING IN THE PAPER

As you can imagine, knowing this information *before* you turn in the assignment would be extremely helpful to you.

> If the instructor makes their grading rubric available to students before the essays are due, take advantage of this policy! If not, ask politely if they will make it available to students.

Having this information will help you understand how your instructor will score your writing. The rubric will indicate which sections or elements of the paper your instructor deems most important, and thus which aspects should receive the biggest portion of your time and attention.

AFTER RECEIVING YOUR PAPER WITH ITS SCORE

Don't simply look at the score and put the paper away. Always read over your instructor's comments and see where you lost the most points. Doing so is one of the most helpful ways to improve your writing.

Many different types of rubric exist, with an infinite number of scales and methods instructors may use to score student work. Clearly we cannot cover all of them in this book, but on the following pages you will find two of the most common types of rubrics: the category points system rubric and the grid rubric.

CATEGORY POINTS SYSTEM RUBRIC

This type of rubric allows students to earn points based on the different parts of the paper, which the instructor tallies to determine the paper's final score. Most instructors who use this type of format write comments in the blank spaces to explain the score and offer constructive feedback to the student. See, for example, a sample list of rubric categories below. Notice each category lists the potential points that the student can earn, for, say, thesis statement versus body paragraphs, etc.

1. INTRODUCTION: Introduces the topic to be discussed, immediately engages reader's interest, and leads reader to the paper's thesis

/15

2. THESIS STATEMENT: Well-written, specific, and clear thesis statement that contains how and/or why element, remains present throughout the essay, directing its content

/10

3. BODY PARAGRAPHS: Contain clear topic sentences that assert each paragraph's claim, remain focused throughout, include citations of clear, relevant examples and/or evidence, and expressly explain how/why the evidence presented illustrates his claim

/30

4. CONCLUSION: Restates the paper's thesis and ties together the paper's claims.

/15

5. ORGANIZATION: Well organized and unified, contains clear evidence of logic and transitions between ideas

/15

6. MECHANICS AND STYLE: Employs a formal, academic tone, uses good syntax, has no spelling/grammatical errors, has effective word choice and varying sentence structure

/15

THE CHART OR GRID RUBRIC

With this grading tool, the instructor may write comments to the student in the appropriate box, or the rubric may contain preprinted comments within the box. The instructor then circles which comments apply to the student's work. The instructor may also simply check which box indicates the essay's level of mastery in that particular criterion area. (For example, a paper deemed "good" in citation format would receive a check mark in the *B* box in the citation column).

Note that in this rubric, all categories receive equal weight, whereas in Rubric 1, the instructor gives the most weight to the body paragraphs. For an example of a grading rubric, see Appendix D.

Grade	Essay Clearly Addresses Prompt and Stays on Topic	Essay Adheres to MLA Grammar, Spelling, and Punctuation Rules	Essay Demonstrates Marked Critical Thinking and Reasoning Skills With In-Depth Analysis	Essay Cites Credible, Academic Sources and Follows the Conventions of MLA Citation Format
A (100–90) Excellent				
B (89–80) Good				
C (79–70) Fair				
D (69–60) Needs Improvement				
F (59 and below) Not Yet at the Passing Level				

SOME FINAL NOTES ON WRITING

Remember, no writer is perfect—not Shakespeare, not Faulkner, not Tolkien, not Rowling, and certainly not you or I, so as you proceed in your classes, strive not for perfection but for *improvement*.

Writing is a skill that can never be completely mastered, but, to me, this is one of its best attributes: There is always more knowledge to acquire. Learning to communicate effectively through your writing is a lifelong pursuit, but it is one that is well worth the time and effort because it pays off again and again, often in unexpected ways.

Below, you will find some of the best quotes on writing, quotes that reveal something about the very nature of writing and how to view and approach it, whether you are a beginner or a master.

> *"The scariest moment is always just before you start. After that, things can only get better." —Stephen King*

> *"Writing is an exploration. You start from nothing and learn as you go." —E.L. Doctorow*

> *"I believe that man will not merely endure: he will prevail. He is immortal, not because he alone among creatures has an inexhaustible voice, but because he has a soul, a spirit capable of compassion and sacrifice and endurance. The poet's, the writer's, duty is to write about these things." —William Faulkner*

> *"Don't get it right, just get it written." —James Thurber*

> *"The worst enemy to creativity is self-doubt." —Sylvia Plath*

I hope you find that these quotes will inspire and encourage you in your pursuit of the craft of writing. If you would like further resources on writing, see both the Works Cited page and the Suggested Reading list provided at the end of the book.

Best of luck in all your future writing endeavors!

Suggested Further Reading

Bradbury, Raymond. *Zen in the Art of Writing: Releasing the Creative Genius Within You*. Bantam, 1992.

Cameron, Julia. *The Artist's Way: A Spiritual Path to Higher Creativity*. New York: Penguin Putnam, 2002.

Goldberg, Natalie. *Writing Down the Bones: Freeing the Writer Within*. Shambhala, 2005.

Graff, Gerald & Cathy Birkenstein. *They Say, I Say: The Moves That Matter in Academic Writing*. W.W. Norton, 2006.

Heffron, Jack. *The Writer's Idea Book: How to Develop Great Ideas for Fiction, Non-Fiction, Poetry, and Screenplays*. Writer's Digest, 2000.

King, Stephen. *On Writing: A Memoir of the Craft*. Pocket Books, 2000.

Maitland, Sara. *The Writer's Way: Realize Your Creative Potential and Become a Successful Author*. Barnes & Noble, 2006.

MLA Handbook for Writers of Research Papers. Modern Language Association of America, 2009.

Rico, Gabriele. *Writing the Natural Way*. Penguin Putnam, 2000.

Robinson, Andrew. *The Story of Writing: Alphabets, Hieroglyphs, and Pictograms*. Thames & Hudson, 2001. Print.

Strunk, William, and E. B. White. *The Elements of Style*. Allyn and Bacon, 1999.

Truss, Lynne. *Eats, Shoots and Leaves: The Zero Tolerance Approach to Punctuation*. Penguin, 2003.

Zinsser, William. *On Writing Well: The Classic Guide to Writing Nonfiction*. HarperCollins, 2006.

APPENDIX A

Essay-Writing Timelines

SUGGESTED WRITING TIMELINE FOR THREE-DAY DEADLINE

If you have fewer than three days to write your essay, compress the timeline accordingly. If you glance at the steps below, you will hopefully notice all the work required will be difficult to handle in fewer than three days, and indeed you are right. It usually takes at least three days to write a strong essay, so I recommend you give yourself at least that much time.

DAY ONE

- Read the prompt carefully; circle keywords or terms such as "analyze," "compare/contrast," or "evaluate."
- Rewrite the prompt in your own words, and compare your version to the actual prompt to make sure you understand it.
- Brainstorm and/or freewrite for fifteen to twenty minutes (repeat if necessary).
- Write a skeleton outline, or compose at least one body paragraph.
- Review the selection(s) you must write about in the essay, and reread all notes you took; write down any ideas that come to mind as you read.
- E-mail or call your instructor and request that she read over your rough draft.

DAY TWO

PART I

- Reread the outline or body paragraph(s) you composed yesterday.
- Begin writing the body paragraphs, the introduction, or the conclusion paragraph—whichever element of the essay you feel most comfortable writing. Make yourself write until you have a good-sized rough draft (preferably three-fourths of the word count of the assignment but at least half).
- Print, and then take a break!

PART II

- Read your draft from beginning to end, and make any necessary changes.
- Write down any concerns or questions you have for your instructor.
- Discuss the essay with your instructor, and take notes on her suggestions.
- Immediately sit down and incorporate her suggestions into the paper.

DAY THREE

- Print the essay, and read it; note any changes you want to make.
- Enter these changes in your electronic version.
- Reprint and reread one last time, making any necessary changes.
- Print the edited version, and turn it in.
- Make a quick note of your process on the essay (the order in which you wrote it, what was stressful or not for you, and what you would do differently next time).

When the instructor returns your essay, always read her comments. Use this feedback to improve in your next assignment. If you are not pleased with your grade or have any questions at all, visit the instructor and politely ask for clarification on comments or grading.

SUGGESTED RESEARCH PROJECT TIMELINE FOR TWO-WEEK DEADLINE

WEEK ONE

PART I

- Follow the three-day timeline outlined on the previous pages.
- Get approval of your topic and perspective from your instructor.

PART II

- Write your research question(s).
- Make your keyword list.
- Go to your college or university library's online catalog and database, and search for articles and books. (Be sure you use the types of sources your assignment requires.)
- Save *all* your findings, and e-mail them to yourself.
- Select which sources to read, and incorporate them into your essay.
- Go to your college or university library, and get your books; print or save articles you plan to read.

WEEK TWO

PART I

- Make an appointment with your instructor to discuss your project thus far.
- Immediately incorporate his suggestions.
- Read and take notes on selected sources. (Follow SQ3R, or use a Research Template.)
- Tie their ideas to yours. (Formulate your response to them: *Yes*, *No*, or *Maybe*?)

- Select the best quotes to illustrate your points, and insert them into your essay.
- Write down any concerns or questions you have for your instructor.

PART II

- Discuss your own writing and the sources you found with your instructor; take notes on any suggestions offered.
- Immediately sit down and incorporate these suggestions into the paper.
- Print the essay, and read it; note any changes you want to make.
- Be sure your quotes flow well in the paper (tie them to your ideas and fully explain them).
- Enter any changes into your electronic version.
- Create a Works Cited page.
- Check all citations, and be sure they adhere to your assigned format style (MLA, APA, or Chicago).
- Reprint and reread one last time; double-check grammar, spelling, punctuation, and all citations.
- Print the final version, and turn it in.

SUGGESTED RESEARCH PROJECT TIMELINE FOR ONE-WEEK DEADLINE

Though some professors may only give a week and a half to write an essay, most instructors allot two weeks or more. Therefore, I do *not* recommend you spend only one week on a collegiate research paper. However, if unforeseen circumstances arise and you have no other choice, see the suggested timeline below. You'll see it's quite a bit to handle in such a short amount of time, so use it only as a last-resort option.

DAY 1

- Follow the three-day timeline outlined on the previous pages. This accelerated schedule will require you to complete all tasks within this timeline within Day 1.
- Be sure your instructor approves of your topic and perspective.

DAY 2

- Write your research question(s).
- Make your keyword list.
- Go to your college or university library's online catalog and database, and search for articles and books. (Be sure you use the types of sources your assignment requires.)
- Save *all* your findings, and e-mail them to yourself.
- Select which sources to read, and incorporate them in your essay.

DAY 3

- Go to your college or university library, and get your books; print or save articles you plan to read.
- Read and take notes on selected sources. (Follow SQ3R, or use a Research Template.)

DAY 4

- Tie their ideas to yours. (Formulate your response to them: *Yes*, *No*, or *Maybe*?)
- Select the best quotes to illustrate your points, and insert them into your essay.
- Print the essay, and read it; note any changes you want to make.
- Make an appointment to meet with your instructor; write down any questions/concerns you have.

DAY 5

- Meet with your instructor; take notes on any suggestions or feedback.
- Incorporate all instructor suggestions.
- Be sure your quotes flow well in the paper (tie them to your ideas and fully explain them).
- Reread your essay, and make note of any changes you need to make.

DAY 6

- Enter any changes into your electronic version.
- Reprint and reread one last time; double-check grammar, spelling, punctuation, and all citations, and note any necessary changes.
- Create a Works Cited page. Check all citations, and be sure they adhere to your assigned format style (MLA, APA, or Chicago).

DAY 7

- Do a final read-through; double-check all citations.
- Print the final version, and turn it in.

APPENDIX B

Sample Student Essay with Instructor Comments

I recommend reading the essay by itself first—without the instructor's comments. See if you can tell where the student exhibited strong writing skills and where you would offer suggestions for improvement. Then, read it again along with the instructor's feedback. Don't worry if your feedback is not exactly like the instructor's; the example is included to give you an overall idea of the type of feedback you may receive from your instructors.

Try for a snappy, relevant title.

Robin Gummo

Professor Brown

English 1310

The Modernization of Shakespeare

Good—you immediately cite the titles of works you will examine.

Replace banned words (such as "you" and "today's world") and specify vague pronoun references

Set up this theme. Your topic: father/daughter relationships in the texts.

Where is your thesis?

To modernize a 16th century Shakespeare play, you need to have a perfect blend of both similarities and differences, making sure to include elements of both worlds. This is what they did in William Shakespeare's *Taming of the Shrew* and *10 Things I Hate About You*. Many of the characters and much of the plot from *Taming* are modernized into the teen world of the late 1990s so that people can relate Shakespeare's play to today's world. One of the most important elements in both stories is the relationship between the father and daughter characters. *Taming of the Shrew* and *10 Things I Hate About You* are very similar in many ways that they deal with this theme, but they also have minor differences, too.

A major difference between Mr. Stratford and Baptista is that Baptista seems less protective of his daughters. When Baptista meets Petruchio (Katherina's suitor), he only speaks to him for a few minutes and is ready to marry her off to this guy he just met. Mr. Stratford, on the other hand, scrutinizes his daughters' dates carefully, and they are just dating!

Good topic sentence here

Another major difference between these two texts is the motivation of the fathers. Baptista in the play seems more like he wants to get rid of the girls and sell them off to the highest bidder than to actually help them be safe and happy. Elizabeth Dreher actually calls Baptista a "mercenary father"! She says, "Shakespeare's mercenary fathers, like Baptista and Polonius, are more coldly calculating. They see their daughters merely as valuable objects and symbols of their power, using them to aggrandize themselves politically or economically" (166). Baptista likes Petruchio instantly because he knows he comes from money.

This is a good quote choice, but comment on it. You agree with Dreher? Why or why not? Also, provide evidence for the final statement.

Baptista's selfishness comes to haunt Kate. Shakespeare foreshadows her horrific ending when he has Petruchio say, "I come to wive it wealthily in Padua; if weathily, then happily" (I.2.74-75). When his friend Hortensio tries to tell him what a "shrew" Kate is, he scolds him, "Hortensio, peace! Thou know'st not gold's effect" (I.2.92). This is no coincidence. Baptista wants to sell off his daughters, so who does he attract? A man who just wants to marry for money. Petruchio definitely proves to be a jerk in the way he treats Kate. He starves her, deprives her of sleep, and even beats the servants in front of her. He also humiliates her at her wedding.

This is an interesting point, but rephrase the sentence to make clear the connection you see between Baptista's selfishness and Kate's "horrific ending."

Tie this information about Petruchio's actions to your topic: father/daughter relationships.

Specify your point: The father's motivation is important in _____?

Although you could argue that both father figures desire to protect their daughters, the different texts really show how important the dad's motivation is. Baptista's desire to protect is really motivated by hunger for power and greed; he sees his girls as valuable objects he can sell. Sarah Hamilton argues that Baptista is like King Lear: "Above all, each man values reputation and status and

These are excellent quote choices, but be sure to comment on your scholars' ideas. Explain how they relate to yours. For example, what is this "telling look" to which Hamilton refers?

eschews any word or act that reflects badly on his public image, and the shallowness of their outlook is revealed by the presence of a sister who is the favored daughter's temperamental opposite" (93). She also points out that the pairing of sisters is not common in his plays; usually the female characters have a cousin or friend, and if she has a sibling, it's a brother. So the fact that there are two sisters is really important. She says the "juxtaposition of opposites provides a telling look at the father-daughter relationship" (94). However, Mr. Stratford's motivation is just to protect his daughters from danger and trouble. He wants to make sure they get the best in life that they can, and he sees boys as being a threat to their futures. He doesn't want his daughters to end up like the girls he sees in his practice who are young and pregnant and have no options left.

Formalize tone (ex: "the whole taming theme").

The whole "taming" theme, which of course is really important to the play's meaning, is somewhat carried over into the movie, though not as strongly as it was in the play. Since the movie is modern, they had to tone it down a little since we don't really believe in women needing to be "tamed" anymore. Although many scholars argue that in the play, Katherina is not tamed, it is clear she is when she makes her final speech. Some people, like scholar Sarah Hamilton, say that Petruchio understands

Kate and is good and helpful to her. Penny Gay, however, agrees ~~with me~~. She says that *Taming* is really just "A story in which one human being starves and brainwashes another, with the full approval of the community … . *The Taming of the Shrew* argues that the cruel treatment is for the victim's good" (86).

~~I think~~ this shows a lot about the differences in our society versus Shakespeare's. Kat in the modern adaptation, is not at all tamed. We can see with these different motivations that the modern father, Mr. Stratford, truly wants the best for his girls and wants to protect them and help them have a great life, even if he does go too far with his rules. This motivation leads to a happy ending for Kat and helps her avoid the whole "taming" fate that Shakespeare's character Kate has. Kat ends up with this great guy who really cares about her, she gets to go off to college, and she finally reconciles with not just her sister but her dad, too. The last thing we see of her is her happy embrace with Pat next to her cool car (which contains a guitar he just bought her!), knowing her future is safe. She playfully scolds Patrick a little to let him know she is still Kat, after all, but he is fine with it; he kisses her to show he likes that she is this way, and he wants her for who she is, not just so he can show off how he tamed her. There is no big speech where she denounces the way she used to be, no big gesture of obedience to Patrick or bowing to his wishes, like Katherina does in the play. I think the film leaves this out to show that now we see that women don't need to be tamed; they just need to be allowed to be who they are, and when they have that freedom, then they will be their true selves.

Remove references to yourself in the essay.

Again, insert your own evidence here to either support or refute your scholars'.

Define your language. This = ____? The "differences" in the societies as revealed by these texts are ____?

Good—this statement gives you a point to argue.

It's a good idea to address the final images we have of the characters; now tie these respective endings to each character's relationship with her father.

Define. The "huge role" they play is ___? Clarify: Why should readers consider this role?

Don't begin a conclusion paragraph with "in conclusion."

Tie together your claims to illustrate what this important role is that you see fathers playing in the texts and why it is of importance to readers.

Where is the Works Cited page?

The differences in the film and play's father figures show ~~what a huge~~ role they play in their daughters' endings, and ~~I think~~ this is something important for readers to consider.

~~In conclusion,~~ *Taming of the Shrew* and *10 Things I Hate About You* are very similar but do share some differences. ~~The modern adaptation of *Taming of the Shrew* kept the same characters and some of the same themes but the filmmakers added some more modern elements. These new modern elements make the story more understandable to a modern audience; and they also reveals to us the major differences in the time periods about attitudes about the value of daughters to their fathers and the important role fathers play in the lives and happiness of their daughters and what ultimately happens to them in life.~~

To download this student's final draft and the instructor's comments, go to www.writersdigest.com/essential-college-writing.

APPENDIX C:
Sample Essay Prompts

See below for examples of writing prompts from several different college-level classes. Granted, each instructor is different, and you may receive prompts that look absolutely nothing like these. However, these examples are meant as just that—*examples*—to give you an idea of the types of prompts you *might* encounter . . .

SAMPLE WRITING PROMPT #1:
ENGLISH CLASS

Instructions: Write a 1,000-word argumentative essay on **ONE** of the three topics listed below.

IMPORTANT DUE DATES:

- Monday, Nov 3: 1st Rough Draft Due (at least ¾ of the word count); Peer Review
- Wednesday, Nov 5: 2nd Rough Draft Due (full word count); Peer Review
- Monday, Nov 10: Final Draft Due; submit a copy to Turnitin.com by 5:00 p.m.

REQUIREMENTS:

- Final draft should be turned in inside a folder; behind your final copy should be the rough drafts and peer

review sheets completed in class, thesis/plan, and
any brainstorming/freewriting
- Double space, use 12-pt, Times New Roman font
- Number the pages
- Give it a pertinent, interesting title
- <u>Include a Works Cited Page</u> at the end of the document—use MLA style

TOPICS

TOPIC CHOICE 1: ENDINGS?

Choose one of the primary fairy tale texts from in-class readings and examine two or three of its more modern (19th-, 20th-, or 21st-century) retellings.

Focus specifically on each tale's ending and *compare/ contrast these endings to discuss how each conveys a different message or "moral" to the reader.* Address, too, which tale (in your opinion) has the most effective or satisfying ending and explain why you think so.

TOPIC CHOICE 2: ARCHETYPES?

Carl Jung defined an archetype as "a universal and recurring image, pattern, or motif representing a typical human experience" (16). Thus, archetypes are patterns and behaviors, primordial images, that form an intrinsic part of our psyche and social systems. The archetypes of the hero, villain, and monster specifically have enjoyed a lengthy history of development, appearing frequently in both film and literature.

Select one of these archetypes (hero, villain, or monster) and a representative text or texts in which to discuss its manifestation(s). You may select up to three texts to discuss, *but no more than three*. At least one of the texts should include assigned course readings.

For example, you may choose a text and its retelling (such as Homer's depiction of Odysseus versus Tennyson's of Ulysses or Homer's idea of Penelope versus Parker's, etc.).

You may also choose two unrelated texts and compare/contrast the characters to determine the nature of the heroic, villainous, or monstrous depicted.

TOPIC CHOICE 3: THE EVOLUTION OF THE HEROIC?
Scholars disagree on whether the ideas and depictions of heroes have truly developed and/or evolved over the course of the centuries. While some theorists believe the hero and our notions of the heroic have indeed dramatically changed with time, others argue the reverse: that is, these readers believe our idea of a hero in AD 2022 is not substantially (if at all) different from earlier writers' ideas of it in, say, Homer's time, approximately 8th-century BC.

Take a stand on this issue; argue whether our idea of the hero has evolved, devolved, or remained largely unchanged—and illustrate HOW, exactly, it has evolved or not.

As evidence and illustration of your viewpoint, *use at least two representative texts from each time period*—at least one from assigned course readings.

SAMPLE WRITING PROMPT # 2:
HUMANITIES CLASS

DUE DATE: Tuesday, April 5, both to me and to Turnitin. com by the <u>beginning</u> of class.

INSTRUCTIONS: Write a 1,000-word argumentative essay on **ONE** of the topics listed below. Be sure to follow all instructions and turn in on time both the printed and electronic copies of your essay.

REQUIREMENTS:

- Turn in the final draft inside a folder, along with your signed peer review sheets, outline, and brainstorming/ freewriting
- Double space
- Use 12-pt, Times New Roman font
- Black ink only
- Number ALL the pages EXCEPT the first
- Title it—Do NOT call it "Paper 3"
- Use at least three sources and cite in MLA style

TOPICS

A. FICTION INTO FILM: "WHERE ARE YOU GOING, WHERE HAVE YOU BEEN?" AND *SMOOTH TALK*
Choose ONE of the following prompts.

   Include in your essay examples from **BOTH the film and the short story** and make clear the source (film or short story) of each example to which you refer.

1. *Compare/contrast the depiction of Arnold Friend in the short story versus the film adaptation.*

Address in your discussion the implications of changes to his character. Explain how/why changes in the filmic depiction of Arnold alter the reader/viewer's understanding of the overall "message" of the film versus that of the short story.

2. *Compare/contrast the endings of the short story and film.*

Your essay should include answers to the following:

- Clear explanations of each ending (Rape? Murder? Etc. . . .)
- How—specifically—each ending impacts the viewer's perception of the overall "meaning" of the short story or film

3. *Discuss the importance of Connie's relationship with her mother in both the short story and film.*

In your answer, account for any differences in the film version and explain their significance.

4. *Discuss the use of symbolism in both the film and short story.*

Your essay should include the following:

- Cite clearly each symbol the essay will discuss.
- Address how—specifically—each symbol contributes to viewer/reader understanding of specific scenes, lines, characters, and the overall story.

5. *Explain why Connie agrees to go for a ride with Arnold Friend.*

Your answer should include the following:

- Does Connie recognize him as a villain? How do you know?

- Do her actions in any way suggest she admires him and the attention he gives her? If so, does that imply she went with him of her own free will?

B. TELEVISION AND FILM STUDIES:

All essays must include examples from the film and/or television program as support for your contentions.

Genre:

Choose at least TWO (but no more than three) TV programs *or* films from a particular genre (situation comedy, western, crime drama, soap opera, action/adventure, game show, talk show, reality show, etc.). *Write an essay that proposes the defining characteristics of the genre.*

Some of the many questions to consider include:

- What do the programs or films have in common?
- What are the situations around which they are built?
- How can these situations be categorized?
- How/Why are the chosen programs/films representative of the genre?

Include the following in your essay:

- Clear definitions of any terms you introduce
- Specific, relevant examples to illustrate these characteristics
- Clear explanations of the effects of these characteristics—in other words, clearly <u>address WHY the characteristics you propose are the defining ones of the genre</u>

Sex and Gender: Choose either Option A or B

A. Choose TWO television programs or films from any genre and *ANALYZE the sexual and/or gender behaviors, values, and attitudes presented.*

B. Watch a particular television network for at least three hours. *ANALYZE the gender and/or sexual behaviors, values, and attitudes presented* in the TV programs and advertisements that appear during the three-hour period.

Use information from the in-class readings, in-class discussion, and especially the TV viewing to support your conclusions.

Essays from either option A or B should include the following:

- Clear identification of the specific behaviors and/or attitudes the essay will discuss
- Specific, relevant examples from the program(s) or ad(s) to support your claims
- Explanations of how/why the shows/ads present these behaviors and/or attitudes in the manner they do. In other words, what impact might this depiction have on audience views of the nature of sex and/or gender?

MARRIAGE:
Choose TWO television programs or films that depict the lives of married couples. *ANALYZE and compare/contrast the depiction of marriage offered in each film/program. How does the show or film define the role of husband? The role of wife? Why?*

You may, for example, choose two contemporary shows or films and compare/contrast their depictions of marriage. Another option would be to select a TV program or film from an earlier decade and compare it to a contemporary one.

If you choose the latter option, discuss whether the depiction has evolved, devolved, or remained intact. Possible examples include: Ward and June Cleaver (*Leave It to Beaver*) vs Homer and Marge Simpson (*The Simpsons*), or Lucy and Ricky Ricardo (*I Love Lucy*) vs Dharma and Greg Montgomery (*Dharma and Greg*).

The essay should include the following:

- Clear identification of the couples the essay will discuss; be sure to include the title(s) of the films or programs that depict them
- Specific, clear claims about each film's or show's depiction of marriage, including the assumed role of each spouse within the marriage (Equals? Dominant? Submissive?)
- Relevant examples from the films or programs to support your claims
- Explanations of how/why the films or shows present marriage in the manner they do—in other words: What impact might this depiction have on audience views of the nature of marriage?

You may also design your own topic, but **BE SURE TO GET MY APPROVAL BEFORE YOU BEGIN!!!!**

SAMPLE WRITING PROMPT #3: PHILOSOPHY CLASS

Some individuals claim that each person is solely responsible for what happens to them, meaning that we can and do possess the power to rule over and create our own lives. Other people disagree. They argue that external factors are so powerful that they essentially dictate the outcome of our lives. Since we cannot control those events or circumstances, then we cannot possibly control our lives' directions and thus who or what we become.

Assignment:

Are we truly free to make our own decisions about our lives, about who and/or what we become? Or, are we limited in the choices that we can make by the circumstances and events we experience?

Enter this debate by taking a side and explaining why you feel as you do.

Plan and write a multi-paragraph essay (1,000–1,200 words) in which you develop your point of view on the above question. Support your position with reasoning and examples taken from in-class readings as well as your own experiences and observations.

DUE: Thursday, April 5 at the *beginning* of class.

REQUIREMENTS:

- Include references to *at least two* of our in-class readings
- Turn in digitally via Blackboard Dropbox by 5:00 p.m. CST on Thursday, April 5

- Turn in a paper copy—with all pages stapled together
- Include a heading at the top of the first page that includes:
  - Your last name, first name
  - Your class number
  - The days/times of your class
- Use APA citation style
- Double space
- Number the pages
- ONLY turn in Microsoft Word documents—no PDFs
- DO **NOT** E-MAIL ME YOUR PAPER
- DO **NOT** TURN IN A GOOGLE DOCUMENT

SAMPLE WRITING PROMPT #4: U.S. HISTORY CLASS

Compare and contrast the reasons for U.S. entry into WWI versus WWII versus *one* other major war (such as Korean War, Vietnam War, or GWOT).

In your discussion, include whether you think the reasons for entering each war were sound or not—and why.

REQUIREMENTS:

- Cite at least one source from class readings and two additional sources we have not consulted in class to support your view
- Cite evidence and explanation to show WHY you think as you do

- Use Chicago citation style
- Turn in your essay either to me, at the beginning of class, or via our class's Digital Dropbox no later than 5:00 p.m. on October 3
- Turn in your rough draft along with your final draft

DUE DATE: October 3

NOTES:
Do NOT simply rehash in-class discussions or repeat what you heard on the History Channel, in your high school history classes, or at the family table.

Instead, dive into the texts we've studied in class. Then, consult two of your own to DEVELOP YOUR OWN IDEAS AND PERSPECTIVE.

Remember there are no "right" or "wrong" answers here. As historians, it's our job to *interpret* history. However, if you have no evidence or thoughtful explanation to support your point of view, few people will take your ideas seriously, and why should they if you have no support? Everyone has an opinion. Historians have an *educated* opinion based on examination and thoughtful analysis of historic fact. If you wish to earn a high score on this essay, then you will do exactly that: Thoughtfully examine and analyze historic fact to come to your own conclusions.

ESSENTIAL WRITING SKILLS FOR COLLEGE & BEYOND

⟿ APPENDIX D: ⟿

A Sample Grading Rubric

On the following pages, you will find a sample grading rubric.

To review grading rubrics and how they work, see p. 255.

Although each writing instructor will design their own rubric for assessing student writing, the sample rubric included on the following pages will give you an idea of what writing instructors may look for in your work.

You can also use this rubric as a checklist of sorts to guide you when editing/revising your work. Imagine *you* are the grader, charged with the task of evaluating a student's written work. It's your job to ensure the student's future success, so don't let them (aka you!) get away with sloppy, lazy work!

However, please note that all writing instructors do not *necessarily use rubrics.*

Some instructors prefer to grade more intuitively, so if your instructor does not use rubrics, consider asking if they would. If not, don't press the issue, but know that you can still use the rubric yourself as a guide to excellence in writing.

SAMPLE ANALYTIC GRADING RUBRIC (FROM THE UNIVERSITY OF NEW BRUNSWICK)*

WRITING RUBRIC

Date: _____

Rater: _____

Course: _____

Student: _____

CRITERIA	Unacceptable	Acceptable	Target	Exemplary	Score
Logic & Organization	Does not develop ideas cogently, uneven and ineffective overall organization, unclear introduction or conclusion.	Develops and organizes ideas in paragraphs that are not necessarily connected. Some overall organization, but some ideas seem illogical and/or unrelated, unfocused introduction of conclusion.	Develops unified and coherent ideas within paragraphs with generally adequate transitions; clear overall organization relating most ideas together, good introduction and conclusion.	Develops ideas cogently, organizes them logically with paragraphs and connects them with effective transitions. Clear and specific introduction and conclusion.	
Language	Employs words that are unclear, sentence structures are inadequate for clarity, errors are seriously distracting.	Word forms and sentence structures are adequate to convey basic meaning. Errors cause noticeable distraction.	Word forms are correct, sentence structure is effective. Presence of a few errors is not distracting.	Employs words with fluency, develops concise standard English sentences, balances a variety of sentence structures effectively.	

ESSENTIAL WRITING SKILLS FOR COLLEGE & BEYOND

CRITERIA	Unacceptable	Acceptable	Target	Exemplary	Score
Spelling and Grammar	Writing contains numerous errors in spelling and grammar which interfere with comprehension.	Frequent errors in spelling and grammar distract the reader.	While there may be minor errors, the writing follows normal conventions of spelling and grammar throughout and has been carefully proofread.	The writing is essentially error-free in terms of spelling and grammar.	
Development of Ideas	Most ideas unsupported, confusion between personal and external evidence, reasoning flawed.	Presents ideas in general terms, support for ideas is inconsistent, some distinctions need clarification, reasoning unclear.	Supports most ideas with effective examples, references, and details, makes key distinctions.	Explores ideas vigorously, supports points fully using a balance of subjective and objective evidence, reasons effectively making useful distinctions.	
Purpose	The purpose and focus of the writing are not clear to the reader.	The writer's decisions about focus, organization, style, and content sometimes interfere with the purpose of the writing.	The writer has made good decisions about focus, organization, style, and content so as to achieve the purpose of the writing.	The writer's decisions about focus, organization, style, and content fully elucidate the purpose and keep the purpose at the center of the piece.	

* Source: The Center for Enhanced Teaching and Learning at University of New Brunswick
https://www.unb.ca/fredericton/cetl/services/teaching-tips/assessment-methods/grading-rubrics.html

·→· Works Cited ·←·

Allegretto, Sylvia, and David Cooper. *Twenty-Three Years and Still Waiting for Change: Why It's Time to Give Tipped Workers the Regular Minimum Wage.* Economic Policy Institute, July 2014, https://irle.berkeley.edu/files/2014/Twenty-Three-Years-and-Still-Waiting-for-Change.pdf.

Calandrillo, Steve P., and Taylor Halperin. "Making the Minimum Wage Work: An Examination of the Economic Impact of the Minimum Wage." *Stanford Journal of Law, Business & Finance*, vol. 22, no. 2, 2017, pp. 147–187.

Cooper, David. *Raising the Federal Minimum Wage to $10.10 Would Lift Wages for Millions and Prove a Modest Economic Boost.* Economic Policy Institute, Dec 2013, https://www.epi.org/publication/raising-federal-minimum-wage-to-1010/.

Crews, Frederick. *The Random House Handbook.* 5th ed., Random House, 1987.

Dash, Irene G. *Wooing, Wedding, and Power: Women in Shakespeare's Plays.* Columbia UP, 1981.

Dickens, Charles. *A Tale of Two Cities.* Barnes & Noble, 1993.

Dreher, Diane. *Domination and Defiance: Fathers and Daughters in Shakespeare.* Kentucky UP, 1986.

Gay, Penny. *As She Likes It: Shakespeare's Unruly Women.* Routledge, 1994.

Hamilton, Sarah. *Shakespeare's Daughters.* McFarland, 2003.

Heffron, Jack. *The Writer's Idea Book: How to Develop Great Ideas for Fiction, Non-Fiction, Poetry, and Screenplays.* Writer's Digest, 2000.

Jenkins, Harold. "Hamlet and Ophelia." *Interpretations of Shakespeare*, edited by Kenneth Muir, Oxford UP, 1985, pp. 142–160.

King, Stephen. *On Writing: A Memoir of the Craft.* Pocket Books, 2000.

Langis, Unhae. "Marriage, the Violent Traverse from Two to One in The Taming of the Shrew and Othello." *Journal Of The Wooden O Symposium*, vol. 8, 2008, pp. 45–63.

Lynn, Michael, and Christopher Boone. *Have Minimum Wage Increases Hurt the Restaurant Industry? The Evidence Says No!. Cornell Hospitality Report*, vol. 15 no. 22, 2015. pp. 1–15. https://ecommons.cornell.edu/bitstream/handle/1813/71234/Lynn_2015_REV_Have_minimum_wage_increases.pdf?sequence=1&isAllowed=y.

MLA Handbook. 9th ed., Modern Language Association, 2021.

MLA Style Manual and Guide to Scholarly Publishing. 3rd ed., Modern Language Association, 2008.

Pittman, Monique. "Taming 10 Things I Hate About You: Shakespeare and the Teenage Film Audience." *Literature Film Quarterly*, vol. 32, no.2, 2004, pp. 144–152.

Publication Manual of the American Psychological Association. 7th ed., American Psychological Association, 2020.

Shakespeare, William. *Hamlet*. Bantam, 1988.

Shakespeare, William. *Julius Caesar. The Complete Works of Shakespeare*. Edited by David Bevington. HarperCollins, 1992, pp. 1025–1059.

Shakespeare, William. *The Taming of the Shrew*. Bantam, 1988.

Strunk, William Jr., and E. B. White. *The Elements of Style* 3rd ed., Macmillan, 1979.

10 Things I Hate About You. Directed by Gil Junger, Touchstone, 1999.

Thoreau, Henry D. *Walden*. Edited by Jeffrey S. Cramer. Yale UP, 2006.

Truss, Lynne. *Eats Shoots and Leaves: The Zero Tolerance Approach to Punctuation*. Penguin, 2003.

Wessels, Walter John. "The Minimum Wage and Tipped Employees." *Journal of Labor Research*, vol. 14, no. 3, 1993, pp. 213–226.

Zavodny, Madeline. "Why Minimum Wage Hikes May Not Reduce Employment." *Economic Review*, vol. 83, 1998, pp. 18–28.

Index

language use. *See* editing essays; inclusive
language; word choice
learning lab, research help from, 123
less/fewer, proper usage, 208
lists and outlines, 33–36

me/I, proper usage, 208
mental blocks, working through, 48–49
MLA (Modern Language Association)
style, 149, 152–153, 155, 157, 158–161,
163–164
models, student-first vs. scholars-first, 7–8

organizing tips, 99–100
outlines
applications beyond essays, 50
lists and, using, 33–36
sample, 34–36
thesis statement and, 58, 59–60, 62,
63, 67
when to use, chart, 42

paragraphs. *See* body paragraphs; conclusion
paragraphs; introduction paragraphs
paraphrasing vs. quoting, 70–71, 143–145
parentheses ( ), use of, 234–235
peer review, 178–185
being a great peer reviewer, 178–183
being honest, not brutal, 183
"compliment sandwich" and, 183
definition and purpose, 178
examples, 184–185
guidelines for using, 178–183
pointing out good *and* bad, 182
reviewing vs. assessing, 181–182
people-first language, 198–200
personal/reflective essays, 8
persuasive essays, 8
philosophy class, sample writing prompt for,
280–281
P.I.E. (Point, Illustrate, Explain). *See also*
illustrations ("I" of P.I.E.)
about: explanation of, 64–65
checklists, 66–67, 71, 74
"explaining" point and its illustration,
73–76
fact vs. point, 66–68
Grouping/Labeling strategy and,
43–47
"point" definition and examples, 66–68

plagiarism, 253–254
points, 66–68
about: overview of P.I.E. and,
64–65
checklist for, 66–67
defined, 66
examples, 67–68
facts vs., 66
visualizing body paragraphs
and, 65
polishing your essay. *See* editing essays; peer
review; punctuation and mechanics;
revising essays; word choice
post-research, 132–165. *See also* editing
essays; peer review; punctuation and
mechanics; revising essays; word
choice
about: research stages/steps
and, 96
citing sources (*See* citations)
incorporating their ideas with yours
(*See* your ideas and their ideas)
pre-research, 97–106
about: overview of, 97–98; research
stages/steps and, 96
creating binder for research
project, 100
creating specific questions based on
prompt, 101–103
keyword list creation, 104–106
organizing tips, 99–100
understanding the assignment, 99
visiting your professor, 99
professors/instructors
editorial feedback from, 187
essay expectations, 4
perspective of, and essays, 2–3
for research help, 123
sample essay with instructor
comments, 267–270
visiting before research, 99
prompts
addressing, for credible essay, 5
defined, 9
example, illustrated, 10–11
importance of understanding and
following, 9–10
pre-research questions based on,
101–103
reading carefully, 9

     ESSENTIAL WRITING SKILLS FOR COLLEGE & BEYOND